American
Country
Cheese

Laura Chenel and Linda Siegfried

FOREWORD BY Evan Jones

ILLUSTRATED BY Victor Ichioka

ARIS BOOKS

ADDISON-WESLEY PUBLISHING COMPANY, INC.
Reading, Massachusetts   Menlo Park, California
New York   Don Mills, Ontario   Wokingham, England
Amsterdam   Bonn   Sydney   Singapore   Tokyo
Madrid   San Juan

American Country Cheese

*Cooking with
America's
Specialty and
Farmstead
Cheeses*

Library of Congress Cataloging-in-Publication Data

Chenel, Laura.
  American country cheese.

  Includes index.
  1. Cookery (Cheese).   2. Cheese—United
States—Varieties.   I. Siegfried, Linda.
II. Title.
TX759.5.C48C49 1989 641.6′73   88-34410
ISBN 0-201-19662-X
ISBN 0-201-52337-X (pbk.)

Aris Books Editorial Offices and
Test Kitchen
1621 Fifth Street
Berkeley, CA 94710
(415) 527-5171

Text design by Janis Capone
Illustrated by Victor Ichioka
Cover photograph by Patricia Brabant
Food styled by Barbara Berry
Cover typography by Copenhaver Cumpston
Set in 11 point Galliard by NK Graphics, Keene, NH

ABCDEFGHIJ-VB-943210
First printing, April 1989
First paperback printing, March 1990

Only a week after completing the first draft of our book, my co-author, Linda Siegfried, died in an airplane crash. Some of the richest and most memorable times of my life were spent with Linda. We traveled through the United States and Europe, wrote two books, and for several years we cooked, ate, drank, laughed, and played together.

This book is infused with Linda's generous spirit and humorous perspective, her genuine love of life and people.

Except for some minor corrections, our book is unchanged from what we wrote together. Its publication is, for me, a tribute to Linda and a memorial to our friendship. The glow of her smile will forever warm my life.

—Laura Chenel

Contents

Acknowledgments

This book would not exist were it not for all of the cheese makers who agreed to be interviewed. We extend our heartfelt gratitude to those who graciously shared their experience, philosophy, and cheeses. The task of creating this book was vastly aided by our good friend, James Rettinghouse. Many thanks to James for the use of his word processor, his tireless tasting, his enthusiasm, and his endless encouragement.

We are grateful to the participating food professionals, and Michael Clark in particular, who were so generous with their recipe contributions. Our work has been enhanced by the ideas of our friend Penelope Wisner and by her sharp and discerning criticism. Our load was lightened by the numerous recipe testers who contributed their time, suggestions, and support. We thank the people at Creative Property Services, in whose office we wrote most of this book, for their generous support, good humor, and tasting of recipes.

Our thanks to our editor, John Harris, who planted the seed that grew into this book, for his suggestions and support.

A special thank-you to inventive chefs everywhere who are cooking with America's cheeses in new and exciting ways, inspiring us to do the same at home.

After the deaths of Linda Siegfried and James Rettinghouse, the completion of this book became an extraordinary challenge. I could not have done it without the unwavering support of my friend and co-worker, Leslie Litwak. I am grateful to Leslie for generously giving of her time, her boundless energy, and her sharp intellect, as well as her word-processing skill. Others were there for me, too, among them, John Harris, whose empathy and compassion gave me courage; Alex Dei, who contributed research and writing; and Nick Rettinghouse, whose strength and courage inspired me to continue.

Foreword

by Evan Jones

Just a few days ago I received a letter from a Canadian who admitted to being "all confused." As a collector of old menus, he told me, he sometimes came upon the item, Club Cheese, or Clubhouse Cheese. "What is really a Club Cheese?" was his question. His appeal emphasizes the still-mounting interest in cheeses in general, of which many are the creations of young American artisans in rural regions throughout the country. As it happens, the creamy, aromatic substance whose provenance that Canadian correspondent sought is a derivative rather than a unique cheese—it evolved as a mixture concocted in the butler's pantry of New York's Manhattan Club two or three generations ago. The original was a combination of Roquefort, or sometimes Gorgonzola, mashed and beaten with eggs and butter and seasoned with chives and freshly ground pepper. In Boston and other places a similar mélange is known as a "cheese crock."

Club Cheese deserves a moment in history, but unlike the more formal examples that have been pursued in this book, it isn't really a stand-up, carefully matured product. The cheeses and their makers that are profiled here by Laura Chenel and Linda Siegfried are, as the Michelin guides would say, worth the journey. Some of them will surprise even an informed cheese lover—he or she will have reason to be grateful to the authors for ferreting out backroads and following them to the discovery of small, almost unsung dairies where some of the best of America's handmade cheeses are produced.

Not that the team of Chenel and Siegfried was the first to go in search of little-known dairy products. *The Century Cook Book* about a hundred years ago cited domestic adaptations of Camembert, Cheshire, Edam, Gorgonzola, Gruyère, Roquefort, Parmesan, and Stilton as worthy products of American dairymen. A few decades back, the distinguished gastronomic authority, James Beard, traveled through the West with Philip and Helen Evans Brown to find the best of regional Blues, Cheddars, Telemes, and Emmentalers as they are made along the Pacific coast and in the valleys of the Rocky Mountains. I also submitted to the general temptation in my book called *The World of Cheese.* Among my surprises was the discovery in Wisconsin of Herbert Mossholder's one-of-a-kind creamy, supple, highly-palatable Loaf. This is a cheese that combines techniques of Cheddar, Swiss, and the assertive American known as Brick. The original cheese maker on the Mossholder farm in Outagamie County had hired an expert for each of the types to spend one day with him, and then had contrived a tri-part combination. It is one of the interesting cow's milk cheeses that defies the prevailing abundance of those made in large factories.

When I tracked down California's Laura Chenel, who tells in her account of her own business how she went to France to learn more about making chèvre, she was pouring goat's milk into forms in her small dairy room behind a suburban house on Ridley Avenue in Santa Rosa. She may have been, in 1981, the first American of her generation to make available to tyrophiles on both coasts her own crumbly, white, New World cheeses so like those that have been made in Provence and the central highlands of France since the days of Henry IV. Soon after her modest start, her *Fromage Blanc,* Chabis, and a log similar to St. Maure, were found on Alice Waters's menus at Chez Panisse in Berkeley and at Ed Edelman's Ideal Cheese Shop in New York—as well as in restaurants and on food counters in between.

Cheeses such as Laura Chenel's Chèvre are, in many cases, also available by mail because of the bright idea of an energetic Wisconsin college student in 1926. In the village of Monroe, he organized Green County dairymen and sent out across the country flyers praising the high quality of local cheeses. Within ten years Wisconsin cheeses from crossroads dairies had been made available to a direct-mail list of half a million people. Today mail order is a convenient way to keep the family larder supplied with interesting variety.

Laura Chenel has been recognized as the West Coast pioneer whose success encouraged other young people in New England, New York, California, and elsewhere to do surprisingly appetizing things with goat's milk. Some of these are free spirits bent on a simple life and dedicated to the theory that small is beautiful. Camilla Stege in Dixmont, Maine, told me she holds her goat cheese production to two thousand pounds annually, just enough to make a small profit because, as she said, she wants to "keep in touch" with her dozen or so animals. Letty Kilmoyer in Hubbardston, Massachusetts, whose appreciative customers have steadily increased, said that she also wants to control growth so that she'll always know by name every doe, buck, and kid. *Farmhouse cheese,* a term current before the industrial revolution, is a label that suggests how intimate a process the making of cheese is for many of the artisans here cited by the authors.

Ten years ago, if you wanted a farmhouse cheese (no matter what animal contributed the milk), you might have been forced either to make it yourself or to shop for a European import. In the time since, a new appetite for regional cheeses from abroad has been created by a generation of travelers delighted with a kind of eating never before familiar to average Americans. This book provides more proof of how much the scene has changed. It comes alive with the pulse of cheese-making self-sufficiency far removed from corporate industries. *American Country Cheese* is, as well, a sort of testament to the lives of American frontier families and of nineteenth-century immigrants who brought with them specific skills from the Old World.

For the kitchen, the book gathers a chtestomathy of uncommon formulas, chosen for their likelihood of enhancing many recipe files. The following are among them: black bean soup with pumpkin and chèvre, Camembert turnovers, Susan Sellew's Goat Cheese and mushroom loaf, cheese popovers, fig and Mascarpone pasta, Brie pancakes, dried corn and Swiss cheese pudding, Cheddar and oyster pie, a quirkily-inspired breakfast dish of asparagus, boiled eggs, and mold-spotted cheese in a white sauce called Blue Morning. It's a list that tastes as good as the descriptions sound.

In *Chèvre! The Goat Cheese Cookbook,* the authors compiled some excellent recipes for a special cheese. Here, some of the dishes succeed in demonstrating imaginative ways with many varieties and prove that farmhouse products can turn a humdrum meal into a meal worth talking about. I shall leave to the reader to choose the most satisfying.

October 1988

Introduction

Creamy blue cheeses on salads or in sauces for pasta; runny, soft-ripening cheeses spread on crusty bread or crackers; hard, dry cheeses grated over pastas, soups, and risottos; aged, full-flavored semisoft cheeses served with wines or fruit to begin or end a meal. . . . These, and others, are all classic cheese combinations we normally associate with the best French, Italian, British, or other European imports. But every one of these wonderful cheese styles and tastes is available today using superb farmstead or specialty cheeses made right here in America, and that is what this book is all about.

For the two years during which we researched and wrote it, mention of our book about American cheese evoked a wide range of responses. Some people looked askance and, we suspect, chuckled behind our backs. Imagining American cheese as a processed, extruded, packaged cheese food, they wondered what kind of exciting cookbook could focus on that. Others considered us pioneers, exploring new and uncharted territory. They thought only of the exotic little Goat Cheeses and fancy Brie that seem to have suddenly appeared everywhere in the last decade. Reality lies somewhere between the two.

Actually, for well over a century, Americans have been unassumingly producing good-quality, interesting cheeses that would make an epicure's heart sing. Only recently have some received the media and public attention that create the illusion that a phenomenon has suddenly occurred. It is like the old saw of the character actor who, after playing small parts for fifteen years in theater and film, is nominated for an Academy Award and considered an overnight sensation.

It is true that some exotic, new American cheeses have materialized in the last several years, most notably cheeses made from goat's milk. Our 1983 entry into the world of cheese cookery was with *Chèvre! The Goat Cheese Cookbook*. The writing of that cookbook sparked our interest in the American cheese industry as a whole.

Not long after the publication of *Chèvre!*, we noticed our conversations turning to questions such as, "What other cheeses are produced in this country? By whom? Why and where are they making them? Where can we find these cheeses? What can we cook with these cheeses?" We fantasized about poking around forgotten corners of America, searching for regional cheeses that were not available to us locally. And that, among other things, is precisely what we did. Our explorations led to this book, a collection of stories about some of America's cheese makers, their histories and motivations, their cheeses, and our recipes using their cheeses. This is a book about food for people who love food. It is a celebration of the vast array of delicious and wholesome American-made cheeses available to us.

First we had to find these cheese makers. To do so, we obtained lists from every state's Department of Agriculture and mailed over four hundred questionnaires to American cheese companies. The sheer number of practitioners was staggering, convincing us not to attempt to write the *Encyclopedia of American Cheese Makers* but rather to focus on specialty cheese makers, to ferret out representatives of most aspects of the business. Excluded from this book are the large corporate makers. Instead, we examined a range from relatively large co-ops to small-production farmstead craftsmen, visiting over fifty specialty cheese factories to conduct our interviews. Initially we did not necessarily expect to find similarities. However, our interviews revealed some common threads and some attitudes that permeate the business regardless of geographical location or size of production.

Americans choose a career in cheese making for various reasons. For some, it is a family tradition: Kolb-Lena, Plymouth, and Ferrante. For others, cheese is a part of their native culture, loved but not easily available here: Bulk Farms, Italcheese, Sonoma Jack, and Bear Flag. For some, cheese making is an outgrowth of the family farm, an interest in the land, and an expression of a life style: Orb Weaver, Guilford, and Hawthorne Valley. In some instances, co-ops were formed to buy and process milk from regional farmers: Tillamook, Cabot, and Valley View. Recently, some businesses started as investments for foreign money: Auricchio and Besnier. In an industry traditionally dominated by men, a growing number of the newer cheese makers are women: Orb Weaver, Little Rainbow, Laura Chenel's Chèvre, and Mozzarella Company. And more recently, some people consider specialty cheese making an opportunity to make money and do something unusual. These people view it as the latest glamorous endeavor, an attitude manifested by some of those who have contributed to a burgeoning wine industry. We predict that this last category will be the one to increase the most in years to come. Why, all of a sudden, do these people think the time is ripe?

In the last twenty years Americans have been traveling extensively in Europe, partaking of an age-old tradition of eating cheese, and returning home, hearts set upon having access to these products. We have enjoyed an unprecedented influx of European cheese ushered by a stunning marketing and advertising campaign. Concurrently, a growth in the popularity of pizza and Mexican food has increased the quantity of cheese in the average American's diet. Meanwhile, as more wine has become available and consumed, so has wine's natural partner, cheese.

The American dairy industry has launched a full-scale advertising campaign for cheese and all dairy products. Americans are highly receptive to this timely crusade. The catchword, *fitness,* has established itself in our vernacular, bringing with it a concern for fat in our diet. It is judicious, however, to keep this issue in perspective. Dairy products presently account for a mere 12 percent of the fat in the average American's diet, compared with the 38 percent contributed by meat, fish, and poultry, and 40 percent supplied by fats and oils (including butter). The fat content of different types of cheese ranges from 16 to 75 percent and, because cheese is satisfying and filling, one is generally content with just a few ounces at a time. In fact, most of our recipes in this book call for approximately two ounces of cheese per serving.

Dairy products are a good source of calcium, which may help alleviate hypertension and prevent osteoporosis. This concern for health has also prompted the trend toward lighter foods, the consumption of less meat, and the use of alternate sources of protein. However, though health is important, it is only one of the criteria Americans employ in selecting foods, two others being convenience and taste.

We would venture to assert that one component of the new American frontier is that of taste and cooking. The remarkable proliferation of American chefs cooking American cuisine has fostered pride in and appreciation of regional food and inspired new twists on traditional American dishes. These chefs search tirelessly for tasty regionally produced ingredients, including cheese.

A cheese maker's work is long, hard, physically demanding and filled with steam, water, and noise. Yet the challenges in the process, such as ever-changing, somewhat unpredictable, microbiological forces, keep the cheese maker fascinated by the mystery of milk. The challenge is the reward. To complicate matters further, cheese makers must deal with problems in the supply of milk, be it quantity, quality, or price. Sales and marketing, rarely considered important in the past, now loom as significant concerns for members of the industry.

Most foreign governments subsidize their dairy industries and their labor costs are lower, so it has been difficult to compete with imported cheeses. Also, the strength of the dollar in the mid-1980s made the price of European cheese more attractive to the American consumer. The American government uses import quotas in an attempt to equalize the competition. And regulations on labeling and the pasteurization of imported cheeses are now more heavily enforced, thereby restricting some imports. This could encourage American cheese makers to fill the void.

When the Vellas in California, the Steiners in Ohio, and Crowleys in Vermont first made cheese, the landscape surrounding them was dotted with small cheese factories every few miles, each making the same type of cheese. Without the luxury of refrigeration and speedy transportation, cheese, by necessity, was produced close to the milk source. Eventually, efficiency, expediency, and specialization resulted in the demise of most of these small plants. It simply was no longer cost-effective for small plants to produce Cheddar, for example. Today, most of the remaining small facilities in Wisconsin are former Cheddar factories that now produce Brick, Jack, and mostly, Mozzarella. Cheddar must be aged, a costly proposition at two cents per pound, per month, in interest alone on borrowed capital. Milk and labor must be paid for promptly, whether cheese is aged or not, a crippling requirement for many small factories. The cost of money is only one expense. Others include payment for the space in which the cheeses are stored, the refrigeration required to store it, and the labor to tend the maturing cheeses. Mozzarella can be produced, wrapped, and shipped the same day the milk is delivered and, given the extraordinary popularity of pizza, the market for Mozzarella is rewarding. Those who have adapted can continue a career they know and love. Most of the cheese made in this country is produced in large, centralized plants. Yet, our wondrously diverse society allows a market for everything. There is a place and a need for both the mass-produced bulk cheeses and the small-production specialties. The same person who shops for unusual cheese in a specialty shop will, on another occasion, purchase a cheese-filled pizza or burrito.

Much of this book is devoted to delicious recipes featuring the cheeses we discovered. Most of these we developed ourselves; some are contributions from American chefs, many from Michael Clark, a noted chef and caterer who works in Monterey County, California. He is also a good friend. Michael jumped on our bandwagon because, having grown up in England, where the cheese course is traditionally part of the meal, he bemoans America's relative lack of knowledge and interest in cheese. He frequently manages to convince his clients and friends to include cheese in their menus and he especially enjoys inventing recipes using cheese. His generosity in providing us with some of those recipes comes from his genuine interest in the subject.

We discovered that most cheese makers had few, if any, suggestions for cooking with cheese, nor could many offer old family recipes using it. They all eat it out of hand, in sandwiches or, typically, as macaroni and cheese. We wanted the recipes to reflect the cheese maker and the region, and to incorporate local ingredients. Our preference is for fresh ingredients and lighter cooking: salads, first courses, quick and easy preparations, and for irresistible comfort foods. Lacking the opportunity to deal with the subject in depth, we have intentionally omitted any discussion of wine in this book—apart from the occasional reference to a particular type as an accompaniment to one recipe or another.

We have organized the book as a journey from East to West, ending in our own Sonoma County, California. As we wrote, we noted with some frustration the emergence of numerous new cheese makers. Severe discipline was required for us to remain seated at the word processor rather than to venture into the country for more interviews. Had we succumbed to our desires to meet them all now, we might be writing this book through eternity. Temptation was strong, but we respected our original intent to study factories with some track-record or history. Meanwhile, we are already plotting the sequel.

American Country Cheese

For years American cheese makers have been attempting to duplicate European cheeses with American milk on American soil. Many of our native cheeses bear the same names as those from Europe, but are particularly American in their characteristics and flavor. In Europe, a long-standing tradition of producing and consuming cheese, embellished by the extraordinary regional variety, accounts for the vast array of cheeses. Only lately in America has the developing interest in eating cheese inspired American cheese makers to provide more variety to satisfy the demand. What follows is a brief discussion of the cheeses described in this book, a mere sampling of those produced in America.

Primer of American Cheeses

Blue

Numerous variations of blue-veined cheeses made from the milk of cows, goats, or sheep have been enjoyed for centuries. The world's sundry Blue cheeses range in texture from crumbly to creamy, in age from one month to twelve, in size from four ounces to eighteen pounds, and in flavor from mild to quite sharp and tangy. The three oldest and most famous are the French Roquefort, the Italian Gorgonzola, and the English Stilton. Generally, throughout history, the blue-veined cheeses have been eaten by themselves, or with bread or crackers, rather than as ingredients in cooking. Typically they are eaten at the end of a meal, accompanied by nuts and a port, a red wine, or a Sauterne. The recipes in which they have been used tend to be fairly simple: salad dressings and pasta sauces, or with pears in a salad.

TYPE: Mold-ripened; blue-veined
AGE: 3 to 12 months
TEXTURE: Moist; tendency to crumble
SHAPE: Wheels
SIZE: 4 to 5 pounds
DESCRIPTION: Mild to sharp, spicy, tart, rich, somewhat salty; white to light yellow, laced with blue
COOKING QUALITIES: Pronounced flavor; blends well with other cheeses in cooking; recommended for cheese course and salads
PRODUCERS: Maytag; Rogue River Valley

TYPE: Unripened, stretched curd

AGE: 1 to 14 days (the younger the better)

TEXTURE: Soft, moist, chewy

SHAPE: Formed balls

SIZE: Approximately 1 ounce

DESCRIPTION: Fresh, delicate, mild, sweet; white color, often packed in whey or brine

COOKING QUALITIES: Best uncooked in salads and antipasti; marries well with vinaigrettes; melts well on pizza

PRODUCERS: F. Alleva; Ferrante Cheese Company; Italcheese; Mozzarella Company; Mozzarella Fresca

Bocconcini
(*see also* Mozzarella)

Brick,
Muenster

Muenster was first made centuries ago by monks in Alsace, France. The contemporary French version is semisoft, rich, and smooth. At its peak, it has developed a red rind, a lusty, pungent aroma, and a tangy flavor. Traditionally in France it is a table cheese. American Muenster, which is quite different from that made in France, ranges in flavor and aroma from bland, nutty, and mild to pungent and strong. Brick is an American invention, developed in Wisconsin and named for its shape. It is generally sold while still mild and nutty, but can be ripened to an assertiveness close to that of a true Muenster, of which it is a variation or derivation.

TYPE: Bacterial surface-ripened; curds cooked, not pressed
AGE: 4 to 8 weeks
TEXTURE: Smooth, pliable, open texture with small holes
SHAPE: Loaves, blocks
SIZE: 5 pounds
DESCRIPTION: Mild, slightly tart, spicy, nutty; pale yellow with orange coating
COOKING QUALITIES: Melts well; slices well; complements most other ingredients
PRODUCERS: Cabot; Kolb-Lena; Valley View

Brie

This soft, buttery, surface-ripened cheese originated several centuries ago in the Seine-et-Marne region just east of Paris in France. During the 1970s its popularity in America grew to epic proportions, as did the tonnage imported from France to satisfy the American market. The French have traditionally enjoyed it as a table cheese, rather than as a cooking ingredient.

TYPE: Mold surface-ripened
AGE: 21 to 45 days
TEXTURE: Soft and creamy to almost fluid
SHAPE: Round and flat
SIZE: Usually 2- to 4-pound wheels; 1 to 1½ inches thick; approximately 12 inches in diameter
DESCRIPTION: Buttery, rich; milder than Camembert; downy white rind with creamy interior
COOKING QUALITIES: Melts quickly; good choice for cheese course and with apéritifs; spreads well on toast and crackers
PRODUCERS: Besnier; Guilford; Kolb-Lena

Camembert

Although there are indicators that the cheese may have been made previously, legend has it that Camembert was created in the late eighteenth century in the Normandy region of France by a woman named Marie Harel. Today, Camembert-type cheeses are made in other parts of France and in other countries. This soft, supple, surface-ripened cheese is similar in flavor to Brie, but more assertive. The French have regarded Camembert as a table cheese, to be enjoyed with or after salad. In Normandy it is frequently served with local apple cider.

TYPE: Mold surface-ripened
AGE: 21 to 45 days
TEXTURE: Soft and creamy to almost fluid
SHAPE: Round and flat
SIZE: 8 ounces, 1 to 1½ inches thick, 4½ inches in diameter
DESCRIPTION: Nutty, rich flavor; downy white rind with creamy interior
COOKING QUALITIES: *See* Brie
PRODUCERS: Besnier; Guilford; Kolb-Lena

The most widely made and consumed cheese in the world originates from the village of Cheddar in Somerset, England, and dates back to at least the late 1500s. It has been made in America since colonial times. In fact, the first cheese factory in the United States, established in Rome, New York, in 1851, produced Cheddar.

The term *cheddar* also refers to a step in the manufacturing process in which the curds are matted into slabs six inches deep. The name also pertains to a specific size and shape of Cheddar cheese, specifically a wheel fourteen inches wide and twelve inches thick that weighs between seventy and seventy-eight pounds. In English cooking the cheese is traditionally used in Welsh Rarebit and the Ploughman's Lunch (a hunk of Cheddar, pickled onions, chutney, bread, and dark ale). In America it has customarily been served with apple pie and melted on top of hamburgers.

TYPE: Curds cooked, cheddared, and pressed
AGE: 2 to 36 months
TEXTURE: Firm, waxy or crumbly, tightly textured
SHAPE: Wheels or blocks
SIZE: 2 to 80 pounds
DESCRIPTION: Mild to sharp, nutty flavor; white to orange
COOKING QUALITIES: Melts well; slices well when young, crumbles when older; suitable for the cheese course; combines well with other cheeses
PRODUCERS: Cabot; Maytag; Rogue River Valley; Shelburne Farms; Sonoma Cheese Factory; Tillamook County Creamery; Vella

Cheddar

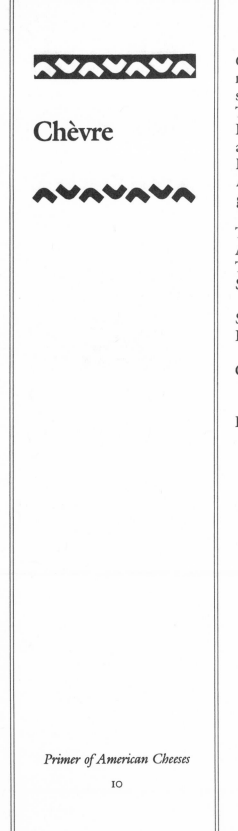

Chèvre

Chèvre is the French word for goat and for the fresh goat's-milk cheese made throughout France in various sizes and shapes. It is sold either plain or coated with herbs or ash. There is limited production of the French type of Chèvre in England, Australia, New Zealand, and America. Traditionally, fresh Chèvre has been considered a table cheese in France and eaten with or immediately after the salad. In America it is often served warmed on salad or used as an ingredient in pasta sauces or on pizza.

TYPE: Goat's milk; unripened, curd uncooked or pressed
AGE: 2 to 21 days
TEXTURE: Moist, soft, spreadable, sometimes spoonable
SHAPE: Varies; packed in containers or shaped into small disks, pyramids, and logs
SIZE: Various; 1 ounce to 1 kilo
DESCRIPTION: Mildly acidic, smooth; white, often coated with herbs or spices
COOKING QUALITIES: Marries well with fruit; suitable for sauces and the cheese board; excellent warmed; for more details *see Chèvre! The Goat Cheese Cookbook*
PRODUCERS: Chenel; Goat Folks; Little Rainbow; Mozzarella Co.; Rawson Brook

A native American cheese, Colby was developed in the late 1800s in Colby, Wisconsin. It is similar to Cheddar in texture and flavor. Colby does not undergo the cheddaring process, that is, the curds are not matted and, unlike Cheddar, the curds are rinsed in cold water. The result is that Colby has a milder taste than that of Cheddar, less acid, and less dense a texture because the curds do not meld together as they would in the early stages of matting, so little holes are common.

TYPE: Curds cooked, rinsed, and pressed
AGE: 2 to 12 months
TEXTURE: Semi-firm, open-textured
SHAPE: Wheels or blocks
SIZE: 2 to 40 pounds
DESCRIPTION: Mild to sharp; white to orange color
COOKING QUALITIES: Melts well; slices well; combines well with other cheeses
PRODUCERS: Crowley; Tillamook County Creamery

Colby

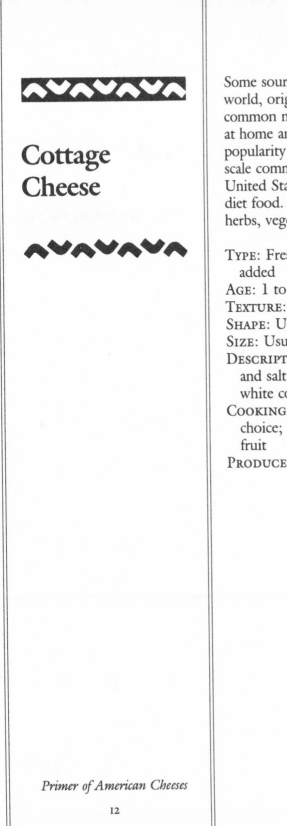

Cottage Cheese

Some sources suggest that this cheese, made throughout the world, originated in Central Europe. Cottage cheese is the common name for a simple, unripened cheese easily produced at home and immensely popular in England and America. Its popularity in America supports a huge business in the large-scale commercial production of Cottage Cheese. In the United States it is eaten as it is and also used extensively as a diet food. It is customarily dressed up by being blended with herbs, vegetables, or fruits.

TYPE: Fresh, unripened, cooked curd, usually with cream added
AGE: 1 to 15 days
TEXTURE: Soft; granular large or small curds
SHAPE: Unformed; packed in containers
SIZE: Usually 8 ounces to 2 pounds
DESCRIPTION: Milky, mild, bland mixture of curds, cream, and salt; may have flavorings such as herbs or fruit added; white color
COOKING QUALITIES: Good for baking; good breakfast choice; suitable for sauces and dips; marries well with fresh fruit
PRODUCERS: Cabot; Nancy's of Oregon

This fresh, simple, rich cheese is one of America's most popular and widely consumed cheeses. An American original, it was invented in New York early in the twentieth century as a version of French Neufchâtel. In the United States, Cream Cheese is customarily used in cheesecake, for spreading on bread, or blending with various flavorings.

TYPE: Unripened cultured milk and cream mixture
AGE: 1 to 14 days (the younger the better)
TEXTURE: Thick, dense, soft, smooth, and spreadable
SHAPE: Unformed; packed in containers or molded into blocks
SIZE: Various
DESCRIPTION: Mild, rich, and creamy; white color; may have added flavorings such as herbs, smoked salmon, fruit
COOKING QUALITIES: Good for baking, frostings, dips and sauces; blends well with other cheeses
PRODUCERS: Mozzarella Co.; Nancy's of Oregon

Cream Cheese

Nancy's Grade A Cultured
Cream Cheese
with Live L.Acidophilus

Ingredients: Pasteurized cream, nonfat dry milk powder, Lecin and L.Acidophilus cultures, salt
Springfield Creamery, Inc.
Eugene, Oregon 97402
Net Wt 8 oz. (227 gm.)

Crottin

This two- to three-ounce goat's milk cheese originated in the Berry district of France, near the town of Chavignol. Though it may be eaten fresh, the French seem to prefer it aged until it is somewhat dry and mellow. In France, it is often warmed over an open fire or grill, or baked and served with greens, as a salad, but most frequently it is served as part of the cheese course.

TYPE: Goat's milk; mold surface-ripened; curds uncooked and unpressed
AGE: 1 to 3 months
TEXTURE: Semisoft
SHAPE: Small rounds, taller than they are wide
SIZE: 3½ ounces; approximately 2 inches tall and 1½ inches in diameter
DESCRIPTION: Complex, nutty, piquant, rich flavor; white interior with a downy white exterior
COOKING QUALITIES: Melts easily; contributes a nutty and goaty flavor to dishes; excellent for the cheese course; slices well
PRODUCERS: Chenel; Goat Folks

This California original was created as a substitute for Parmesan during World War I, when trade with Italy had ceased. It is actually a variation of Monterey Jack that has been aged for a minimum of seven months and coated with oil, cocoa, and pepper to protect it from mold growth while it is aging. Until the 1930s, there were sixty factories producing this cheese in California; presently is made in only two small plants.

TYPE: Pressed, cooked curd; aged
AGE: 9 to 36 months
TEXTURE: Hard, firm, dense; grainy when older
SHAPE: Wheels
SIZE: 8 pounds
DESCRIPTION: Sweet, nutty, rich flavor; light yellow cheese with cocoa-colored rind
COOKING QUALITIES: Excellent grating cheese for pasta, risotto, or vegetables; easily sliced when under a year old; suitable for the cheese course
PRODUCER: Vella

Dry Jack

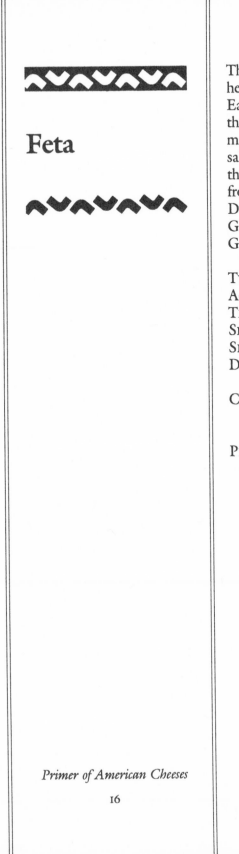

Feta

This is the Greek name for a cheese originally made by shepherds in the mountains of various countries in the Middle East. A white cheese made from sheep's or goat's milk and the only cheese cured in a salt brine, Feta was traditionally made under quite rudimentary conditions. The quantities of salt in this cheese were probably added to preserve it. Today the cheese is produced commercially on a large scale, usually from cow's milk, in numerous countries, including France, Denmark, Italy, Germany, and America. Feta is essential to Greek cookery in such dishes as *spanakopittá, tiropittá,* and Greek salads, and is also used as a table cheese.

TYPE: Uncooked, lightly pressed curd; salt brined
AGE: 1 to 6 months
TEXTURE: Semi-firm and crumbly
SHAPE: Blocks; cubed for brining
SIZE: Usually 1- to 2-pound cubes
DESCRIPTION: Sharp, salty and slightly sour; white color; may be sold in its brine
COOKING QUALITIES: Good in appetizer and salad courses; softens slightly when heated: its salty, acidic, sharp flavor combines well with Mediterranean ingredients
PRODUCERS: Kolb-Lena; Mozzarella Co.; Vella

This supple cow's milk cheese has been made for hundreds of years by farmstead producers in the Aosta Valley of northern Italy. Traditionally it has been used in *fonduta*, a dish similar to the Swiss fondue, as an embellishment for pasta, and as a table cheese. Presently Fontina is produced in Denmark, Sweden, Switzerland, and in America.

TYPE: Curds cooked and pressed
AGE: 2 to 12 months
TEXTURE: Semisoft to semi-firm; smooth and slightly elastic
SHAPE: Wheels
SIZE: 25 to 40 pounds
DESCRIPTION: Delicate, nutty, buttery, honeyed flavor; ivory to straw-yellow color, often with red wax coating; small, gas-formed, round air pockets or "eyes"
COOKING QUALITIES: Melts well; slices well; combines well with other cheeses; acceptable for the cheese course
PRODUCER: Auricchio

See Chèvre; Crottin; Taupinière; Tome

Fontina

Goat Cheese

Primer of American Cheeses

Gouda

This semi-hard cow's milk cheese with a range of flavor from milky when young to sharp when aged originated at least eight hundred years ago in the town of Gouda, near Rotterdam, in Holland. Originally a farmstead cheese, almost all the Gouda sold today is commercially produced and it is made all over the world. Consumed primarily as it is, Gouda possesses excellent melting qualities as well.

TYPE: Curds cooked and pressed
AGE: 2 to 12 months
TEXTURE: Semisoft to firm, supple
SHAPE: Flattened spheres
SIZE: 2 to 20 pounds
DESCRIPTION: Sweet, mild, buttery; pale yellow with red wax coating; may contain spices, such as cumin
COOKING QUALITIES: Slices well; melts well; blends with other cheeses; suitable for the cheese course
PRODUCER: Bulk Farms

An American original similar to Cheddar and Colby, Granular or Stirred-Curd was actually made in America before Cheddar was made. The cheese made by Plymouth and discussed in this book is an example of this type, which is produced commercially in large quantities today. The curds are not rinsed and the cheddaring step is omitted in the process. As a result, the small curd particles do not bond as well as they do in Cheddar, so the cheese has a granular appearance.

TYPE: Cheddar type; curds cooked and pressed
AGE: 2 to 12 months
TEXTURE: Semi-firm, open-textured
SHAPE: Wheels or blocks
SIZE: 2 to 40 pounds
DESCRIPTION: Mild to sharp; ivory to yellow; may contain spices or herbs
COOKING QUALITIES: *See* Cheddar
PRODUCER: Plymouth

Granular or Stirred-Curd Cheese

Gruyère and Emmenthaler

HAWTHORNE VALLEY CHEESE *gruyere*

Made from our cows' fresh raw milk.

HAWTHORNE VALLEY FARM
HARLEMVILLE, GHENT, NY 12075

Gruyère is named for the Swiss village of Gruyère near the French border, where it has been made since medieval times. Today its production is an important industry in both France and Switzerland. Its process is similar to that for Swiss cheese (see page 28), except that it is cured at a lower temperature, so that those holes in cheese, which have been caused by gas that expands when the cheese is curing and are known as "eyes," are smaller, and at a higher humidity so that a dark rind forms. It has a sweet, nutty flavor, sharper than that of Swiss. Traditionally it has been used in fondue in Switzerland, as an all-purpose cooking cheese in France, and as a table cheese. Emmentaler is another of the Swiss cheeses and is named for the Emmental Valley where it was first made. (American producers of the cheese call it Emmenthaler.) It is distinguished by the size of its eyes, which are large—about half an inch to an inch in diameter—and shiny. The cheeses themselves are also large; they can weigh as much as two hundred pounds, but are usually made in wheels that weigh about 160 pounds. This cheese tastes slightly sweeter than does Gruyère.

TYPE: Curd-pressed
AGE: 2 to 6 months
TEXTURE: Dense, smooth, and elastic
SHAPE: Wheels
SIZE: 10 to 15 pounds
DESCRIPTION: Nutty, sweet, mild to full flavor; ivory to yellow; characteristic eyes
COOKING QUALITIES: Melts well; slices easily; blends well with other cheeses
PRODUCER: Hawthorne Valley

This popular cheese was first produced on farms in the vicinity of Monterey, California, in the late nineteenth century. A Scot named David Jacks later produced it on a larger scale to sell it to a greater area than Monterey. Called Monterey Jacks, the cheese was named for him and the shipping point. Over the years, the *s* was dropped from the name. Though this cheese is produced commercially on a large scale throughout America, there are still a few small-scale producers in California who make a superior product. Jack is popular in sandwiches, as a melting cheese (often in Mexican food) and, among the cheese makers themselves, as a table cheese.

TYPE: Curds cooked and pressed
AGE: 1 week to 6 months
TEXTURE: Semisoft, moist, and supple
SHAPE: Wheels or blocks
SIZE: 8 to 40 pounds
DESCRIPTION: Mild, lactic, bland, and buttery; yellowish white color; may contain spices such as garlic and pepper
COOKING QUALITIES: Melts well; blends well with other cheeses; complements spicy flavors
PRODUCERS: Cabot; Rogue River Valley; Sonoma Cheese Factory; Tillamook County Creamery; Vella

Jack

Mascarpone

Originally from the region south of Milan in Italy, this thick, rich, fresh cheese used to be made only in winter because it is so delicate. With improved transportation and refrigeration, it is now made year-round. Mascarpone is a major ingredient in multilayered Italian cheese *tortas* that are made with Gorgonzola, nuts, figs, or basil and in the Italian dessert, *tiramisu*. It can be used much like cream, with fruit or in cakes.

TYPE: Fresh, unripened; made from cream
AGE: 1 to 14 days
TEXTURE: Soft, creamy, spoonable
SHAPE: Unformed, packed in containers
SIZE: 8 ounces to 4 pounds
DESCRIPTION: Rich, fresh, sweet with hint of acidity; creamy white
COOKING QUALITIES: Excellent dessert cheese; marries well with fruit and chocolate; *see also* Cream Cheese
PRODUCERS: Italcheese; Mozzarella Co.

MASCARPONE CHEESE

Ingredients: Pasteurized cream.

MOZZARELLA COMPANY
2944 Elm St., Dallas, TX 75226

Mozzarella

Technically, Mozzarella can only be made with water buffalo's milk, as it was originally; the cow's milk version is known as Fior di Latte. This type of soft, fresh cheese that is native to Southern Italy is known as *pasta filata,* or spun curd, because the curds are warmed and then stretched until they are soft and almost plastic. Traditionally, Italians combine just-made Mozzarella, still warm and dripping with whey, with fresh tomatoes, basil, and olive oil. It has also been used extensively as a cooking cheese because it melts so well.

Today there is a fully mechanized, worldwide commercial production of large quantities of this cheese to supply a huge and growing demand. The commercial product is slightly rubbery, very bland, firmer, and considerably less moist than is the traditional variety. The recent growth in the popularity of pizza has stimulated production of commercial Mozzarella. Nevertheless, it has long been the practice of Mozzarella manufacturers on the East Coast to ship iced curd to tiny *latteria* in metropolitan areas. There the curd is stretched and the cheese can be sold very fresh. Very small, one-ounce balls of Mozzarella are called Bocconcini (see page 5).

Type: Unripened, stretched curd
Age: 1 to 14 days
Texture: Soft, moist, and chewy
Shape: Formed balls
Size: 8 ounces to 1 pound
Description: Fresh, delicate, mild, sweet; white color, often packed in whey or brine
Cooking qualities: Best uncooked in salads and antipasti; marries well with vinaigrettes
Producers: F. Alleva; Ferrante; Italcheese; Mozzarella Co.; Mozzarella Fresca; Rogue River Valley

PASTEURIZED MOZZARELLE   ALLEVA DAIRY N.Y.C. 31-0988

MADE FROM   WHOLE MILK
TO BE WEIGHED   AT TIME OF SALE
BEST QUALITY

Parmesan

True Italian Parmesan, *parmigiano-reggiano,* is one in a group of cheeses known in Italy as *grana* (granular, grain). The cheese was first made near the town of Parma. Manufacture has spread somewhat, but is limited to a legally defined region in north and central Italy and is strictly controlled by the government. *Parmigiana-reggiano* boasts a rich, buttery, sweet, and nutty flavor and a grainy texture. The sixty-five- to eighty-five-pound wheels are aged for between one to three years. In Italy it is usually served either thinly sliced in salads, or with pears and grapes, or grated over soups, pastas, and risottos. American-made Parmesan is usually cured for between ten to fourteen months and is used primarily for grating.

TYPE: Curds cooked, pressed
AGE: 10 to 36 months
TEXTURE: Hard, brittle, grainy
SHAPE: Wheels
SIZE: Various large sizes, between sixty-five and eighty-five pounds
DESCRIPTION: Rich, earthy, somewhat salty, sweet to sharp; pale to deep yellow with a dark, thin rind
COOKING QUALITIES: Easily grated; suitable for the cheese course; blends well with other cheeses
PRODUCER: Auricchio

An Italian *pasta filata* cheese that originated in southern Italy but is presently also being produced elsewhere in Italy and in America, Provolone is an aged Mozzarella given various names for its numerous shapes and sizes. It is often lightly smoked. After it has been cured, it is dipped in wax and hung from the ceiling by twine or raffia to develop further. It is excellent for grating when it has been well aged. Provolone, along with roasted peppers, marinated mushrooms, and pepperoni, is a classic ingredient in Italian antipasti. It is used as a cooking cheese as well.

TYPE: Aged Mozzarella
AGE: A few to 24 months
TEXTURE: Semi-firm; elastic to crumbly
SHAPE: Various, most commonly a large salami shape
SIZE: Various, from a few ounces to two hundred pounds
DESCRIPTION: Mild to sharp or piquant in flavor, smooth, often smoked; creamy white; characteristically waxed and hung with rope
COOKING QUALITIES: Melts well; slices easily; blends well with other cheeses; acceptable for the cheese course
PRODUCER: Auricchio

Provolone

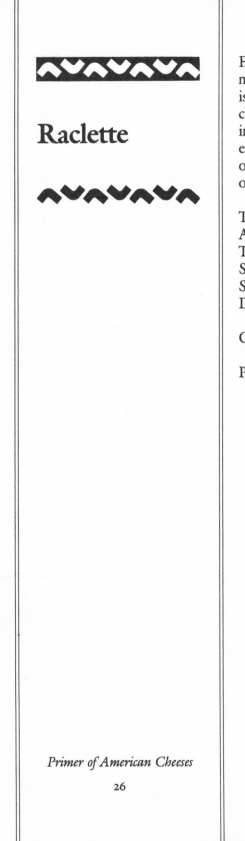

Raclette

From Valais, in Switzerland, south of the Gruyère and Emmental Valley, this cheese is similar in texture to Gruyère but is stronger in flavor and has fewer eyes. A high-altitude cheese, it is made only in spring and fall. It is used primarily in the Swiss dish of the same name, in which cheese is softened in front of an open fire. Slices are scraped off the block of cheese, to be served with small boiled potatoes, pickled onions, and cornichons, and accompanied by white wine.

TYPE: Curd-pressed
AGE: 2 to 6 months
TEXTURE: Semisoft and creamy; rough rind
SHAPE: Wheels
SIZE: 10 to 15 pounds
DESCRIPTION: Sweet buttery flavor; ivory to yellow; occasional small eyes
COOKING QUALITIES: Melts well; blends well with other cheeses
PRODUCER: Hawthorne Valley

HAWTHORNE VALLEY CHEESE *raclette*

Made from our cows' fresh raw milk.

HAWTHORNE VALLEY FARM
HARLEMVILLE, GHENT, NY 12075

Originally made from the whey of Mozzarella, Ricotta (meaning "re-cooked") has a long history. Today it is made throughout Europe and in America, from the whey of various cheeses, with or without the addition of whole milk, or from whole milk entirely. Though similar to commercial Cottage Cheese, its curds are smaller and softer. Ricotta is a popular cooking cheese that may be used in stuffings, fillings, and for baking. In America, it is often eaten directly out of the container, just as it is.

TYPE: Unripened, cooked curd; made from whey and milk
AGE: 1 to 7 days
TEXTURE: Moist, finely granular
SHAPE: Unformed, sold in containers
SIZE: 8 ounces to 3 pounds
DESCRIPTION: Mild, sweet; soft, white curd
COOKING QUALITIES: *See* Cottage Cheese
PRODUCERS: F. Alleva; Ferrante; Italcheese; Mozzarella Co.; Mozzarella Fresca

Ricotta

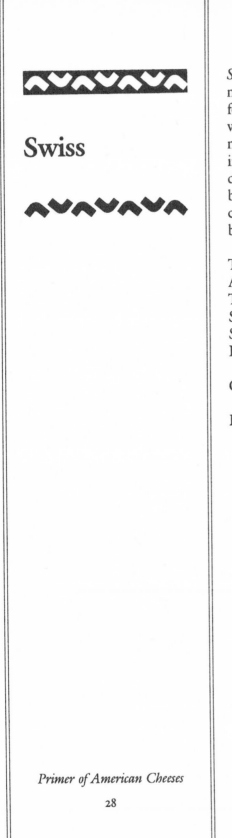

Swiss

Swiss is a generic term for various types of cheeses, originally made in Switzerland, in which gases in the ripening cheese form "eyes." Though these cheeses are copied throughout the world, the exact flavor has never been reproduced. In the mid-nineteenth century, the first Swiss-style cheese was made in America by Swiss immigrants. Today the Swiss cheese produced here commercially is usually in the form of a rindless block that is softer and less aromatic than wheel Swiss. This cheese is used extensively in sandwiches, cooks well, and may be eaten as it is.

TYPE: Curd-pressed
AGE: 2 to 12 months
TEXTURE: Dense, smooth, and elastic
SHAPE: Wheels and blocks
SIZE: 20 to 200 pounds
DESCRIPTION: Mild, nutty, sweet flavor; yellowish-white color; characteristic large eyes
COOKING QUALITIES: Melts well; slices easily; blends well with other cheeses
PRODUCERS: Kidron; Kolb-Lena; Steiner; Sugarcreek

A proprietary goat's milk cheese made by Laura Chenel's Chèvre. The cheese was named in 1983 by a young French employee, *taupinière* being the French word for molehill. This cheese is most appreciated as a table cheese, and lends itself well to cooking.

TYPE: Goat's milk; curds uncooked, unpressed; mold surface-ripened
AGE: 1 to 6 months
TEXTURE: Moist, slightly crumbly, soft
SHAPE: Cylindrical
SIZE: 9 to 10 ounces
DESCRIPTION: Pronounced mild to tangy flavor; mold-covered ash surface with white interior
COOKING QUALITIES: Distinctive; good for the cheese course; flavor intensifies with heat
PRODUCER: Chenel

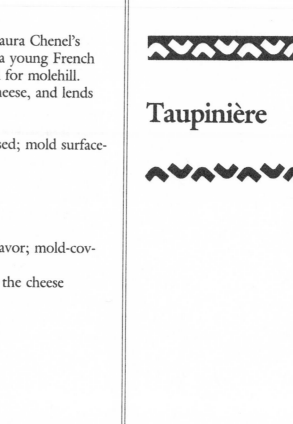

Taupinière

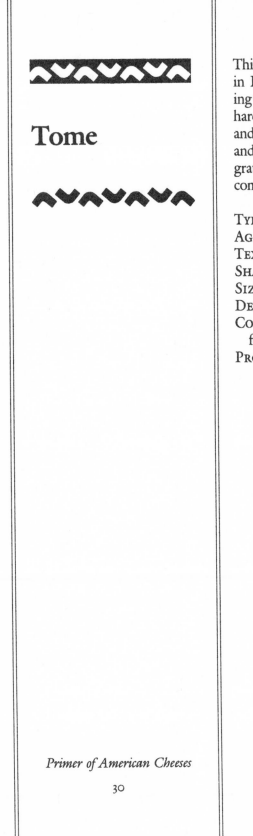

Tome

This is another proprietary cheese developed by Laura Chenel in 1983. Ignazio Vella contributed some helpful manufacturing suggestions. Similar to a Pecorino Romano, this dense, hard cheese has a rich, buttery, nutty flavor at twelve months and, if aged for up to three years, develops an orange hue and a deeper and sharper flavor. Though it is an excellent grating cheese, it is also an agreeable table cheese, when accompanied by a refreshing salad or a hearty red wine.

TYPE: Goat's milk; curds cooked and pressed
AGE: 6 to 36 months
TEXTURE: Hard, dense, and grainy
SHAPE: Wheels
SIZE: 2½ to 4½ pounds
DESCRIPTION: Pungent, rich, nutty; straw yellow color
COOKING QUALITIES: Excellent for grating; recommended
    for the cheese course
PRODUCER: Chenel

This is an original American proprietary cheese from the Guilford Cheese Company in Vermont, inspired by numerous popular fresh cow's-milk cheeses made in France. A molded cheese, it is drier and firmer than Cottage Cheese. It is available plain or with herbs. It may be used in salad dressings, for dessert, or as a breakfast cheese.

TYPE: Unripened, drained curds
AGE: 3 to 21 days
TEXTURE: Moist and closely grained
SHAPE: Unformed
SIZE: 5-ounce containers
DESCRIPTION: Mild, sweet; white, often flavored with herbs
COOKING QUALITIES: *See* Cottage Cheese and Ricotta
PRODUCER: Guilford

Verde-Mont

Suggested Cheese Substitutions

⊨▭▭▭▭▭▭▭▭▭▭▭⊨

Although the recipes in this book were developed to show-case the featured cheeses—most of which are available by mail order (see page 256 for addresses of the cheese maker) if not directly from your local cheese shop—all of our recipes can be made and enjoyed with good-quality substitutions. Ideally, to maintain the distinctive flavor of each recipe, one should substitute, if that is necessary, first with other cheeses from the cheese makers discussed in our book, or other high-quality American specialty and farmstead cheeses, then with imported cheeses, and, as a last resort, mass-produced domestic cheeses, which will also work in many of our recipes. Here is more detailed information on substituting for the cheeses specified in our recipes.

Substituting for Proprietary Cheeses

The cheeses listed below are proprietary originals for which there are no common American-made substitutes. We suggest as substitutes commercially available cheeses that will provide a successful result.

CHEESE IN RECIPE	SUBSTITUTES
Auricchio Fontina; Provolone	Italian Fontina imported Provolone
Bulk Farms Gouda	Jack; imported Gouda
Chenel Taupinière; Crottin Tome	French Bucheron Pecorino Romano
Crowley Colby	mild Cheddar
Guilford Verde-Mont	Farmer's Cheese; Ricotta
Hawthorne Valley Gruyère; Emmenthaler	imported Gruyère imported Emmentaler
Nancy's Cream Cheese	Cream Cheese with "no gum added"
Orb Weaver Cheese	Jack; Gouda; Muenster
Plymouth Cheese	mild Cheddar; Colby
Valley View Muenster; Brick	Havarti
Vella Dry Jack	Parmesan

Substituting for Traditional Cheese Types

This list includes the cheeses mentioned in our book, such as Blue and Camembert, for which you can substitute other, similar cheeses such as those mentioned in our book, other high-quality American cheeses, imported cheeses, or in certain cases, mass-produced American versions. Your local cheese merchant can make suggestions. Remember always to substitute with the best quality, domestic or foreign. (See our Final Note below for a few reservations.)

Blue Cheese
Brie
Camembert
Cheddar
Feta
Goat Cheese, fresh
Jack
Mascarpone
Mozzarella, fresh
Ricotta
Swiss

Final Note

For a few of the cheeses in the second list—Jack, Mozzarella, and Swiss—there are no commonly available commercially produced substitutes that bear a respectable resemblance to the fine examples mentioned in our book or to those from other specialty cheese makers. So, if you can't find a good-quality foreign or domestic Jack, Mozzarella or Swiss cheese, we suggest that you try a different recipe.

The Handling and Enjoyment of Cheese

᠆᠆᠆᠆᠆᠆᠆᠆᠆᠆᠆᠆᠆

Buying

Ideally, one would buy cheese from a well-informed cheese monger at a well-stocked neighborhood cheese shop with a good turnover. Each day the cheeses offered would be perfectly ripe and ready for use that evening. One would feel free to ask all manner of questions and be assured of receiving knowledgeable answers. One could taste any and all cheeses being considered for purchase. Cheeses would be cut to order and suggestions for their use would be offered.

Alas, we do not live in a perfect world and such cheese shops are rare. Most of us must be content to buy our cheese at a supermarket where all too frequently we can expect not much more than a refrigerated case filled with a boring selection of pre-cut, pre-packaged, pre-priced cheeses. There may be an employee behind the counter, but most are insufficiently trained and know little about cheese. Frequently they are not permitted to offer tastes to curious consumers. Some supermarket chains are adding service delicatessens and offering a varied selection of specialty cheeses. May this trend continue!

If you do have the opportunity to inspect a cheese living outside of a plastic wrapper, consider the following: A good cheese invariably looks good. Soft-ripening cheeses should not have dry edges, smell of ammonia, or be concave. Aged cheeses should not be dry or cracked. A high-quality cheese can have a strong aroma and still be delicious. The essential questions to ask are: Does it taste good? Do I like it? Is the flavor of the cheese appropriate for the use I have planned? Elements to consider when tasting cheese include the sodium level, moisture, texture, and acidity. Remember, the mouth only enables us to taste bitter, salt, sweet, and sour. Rely on your nose for the rest. Be sure that the cheese to be tasted is at room temperature so that you may enjoy the most pronounced flavor.

Recently, with the advent of local farmers' markets, some farmstead cheeses have become more readily available. Many cheeses are available by mail-order, as are most of the cheeses discussed in this book. Cheese makers recommend that mail-order purchases be made only during the cooler seasons of the year. You will get a better cheese if you buy it whole. For the larger cheeses, if you are unable to use a whole one, you may consider sharing the purchase with friends.

Storing

If you are fortunate enough to have ready access to cheese, buy only what you intend to use immediately. If you are going to store cheese, wrap it tightly in foil or plastic wrap, then seal it in plastic bags or containers for air-tight protection in your refrigerator. In the case of particularly aromatic cheese, this procedure protects the rest of your food as well. The more moisture in a cheese, the shorter its life will be. The firmer cheeses and Blue Cheese may last for weeks if wrapped tightly in foil. The refrigerator slows but does not stop the ripening process. Cheese will naturally develop mold and its flavor will become more pronounced as it ages. If you cut away and discard the mold, you can still enjoy the cheese underneath. However, soft cheeses that grow mold should be discarded. Frequent changes of temperature are unkind to cheese. Always cut off the portion of cheese you plan to consume and, to keep it better, rewrap the remaining cheese in fresh foil or plastic each time you cut a piece. To ripen a young, soft-ripening cheese further, leave it unrefrigerated, but wrapped, for a day or two.

For those odd bits and pieces of cheese that inevitably remain, we have three suggestions. You can store them in an air-tight plastic container and use them within a week as an addition to soups, sauces, salads, and so on. You can wrap them tightly and freeze for use later. Or you can grate all the little scraps and mix them together with butter or cream cheese, add some brandy or cognac, and allow the mixture to mellow for a few days before using it as a spread.

It is best not to freeze cheese. If you must, be aware that the texture and flavor may change. Make sure that the cheese is in good condition before freezing it. Wrap it tightly in heavy foil and several layers of plastic wrap in order to preserve as much flavor and moisture as possible. Freeze cheese for a maximum of six months. Before using, thaw it slowly in the refrigerator for twenty-four to forty-eight hours.

Serving

To enjoy cheese at its best, serve it at room temperature. For the firmer, denser cheeses this means that they should be removed from the refrigerator several hours in advance; for young, fresh cheeses, an hour or so will do. If you buy your cheese in the morning and plan to serve it in the evening, it probably will not need to be refrigerated. When cheeses are cold, the true depth of their flavors is locked in and their texture is less supple.

Cheese may be eaten for breakfast, lunch, and dinner, at cocktail time, at wine tastings, for dessert, or as a cheese course before dessert. If you are serving cheese just before dinner, offer only small quantities to whet appetites rather than dampen them. For cocktail parties and wine tastings, you can offer more and varied cheeses, as they are a useful foil for the alcohol. The butterfat in cheese counteracting the effects of alcohol helps avoid inebriation.

As Americans produce more interesting cheese, the cheese course is becoming more accepted and even popular. Served alongside or after the salad, cheese aids digestion and cleanses the palate. Offer a selection of at least three or four cheeses, ranging from mild to sharp, soft to hard. Cut and serve only as much as you plan to eat. Wooden planks, wicker baskets, straw mats, and marble slabs are typically used for serving. Garnish the dishes with fresh leaves, herbs, or flowers. Leave some space around the cheeses and provide a separate knife for each one. Pass French or whole-grain bread or unsalted crackers.

We love the cheese course because it is a relaxed moment of conviviality, a time to share impressions of cheese with friends. However, we cannot with any conscience recommend it after a meal of rich and creamy food or one that includes any recipe from this book. In other words, do not paint the lily.

Cooking

The addition of cheese to a dish adds a tremendous amount of flavor and lends interest to other ingredients. Generally, the more aged the cheese, the more flavor it has. A small quantity of well-flavored cheese goes a long way toward converting the mundane to the exciting. Cheese should be at room temperature when you add it uncooked to a dish such as salad. If you forget to remove it from the refrigerator in time, a few seconds in a microwave oven will bring it to room temperature.

To coax the best results from cheese when heating it, bear in mind the following information. In cheese making, the addition of acid to milk entraps the protein molecules. Once milk has become cheese, exposure to extreme temperatures or any further addition of acid can cause these molecules to lose their cohesion and change their structure. If exposed to too high a temperature or too prolonged a cooking time, high-moisture cheese will fall apart and harder cheese will toughen. To avoid such problems, simply remember to heat cheese gently over low heat. When making sauces or soups, use a heavy-gauge pan, grate or cut the cheese into small cubes, add it at the very end, and heat only until the cheese is melted and hot, but not bubbly or boiling. When melting cheese under a broiler, watch carefully and remove from heat when just melted. Microwave cooking of cheese can be tricky. Be sure that all the pieces of cheese are of a uniform size and expose them to only a few seconds at high power. Since an integral part of the cheese-making process is the inclusion of salt, wait until the cheese has been added and then taste before adding more salt.

F. Alleva
Latticini

....

New York City

F. Alleva Latticini

....

New York City

CHEESES: Mozzarella,
  Smoked Mozzarella,
  Ricotta, Manteche,
  Bocconcini
RETAIL SALES: Yes
TOURS: No
MAIL ORDER: Yes

Searching for the great cheese makers of America, one usually travels roads that cross the hills and flatlands of America's agricultural countryside. Not so when one is looking for F. Alleva Latticini (Italian for dairy products). To find F. Alleva, one must travel south from mountainous highrises, through the traffic-clogged narrow streets of Manhattan toward the southern part of that city, deep in the heart of Little Italy, to 188 Grand Street.

In the late 1800s America was blessed by waves of immigrants from all of Europe. This area of Manhattan was to be the new home for many of them from Italy. Along with the desire for a new life, the Italian immigrants, like other ethnic groups, wanted to preserve the culture and tastes of their homeland. Numerous businesses were created to fulfill that desire. Small shops and stores sold many goods made in Italy. Fresh milk products, however, could not be imported, yet they were vitally important to the cooking style so familiar and dear to these new Americans.

Pina Alleva saw a need and decided to fill it. In 1892, Pina, the college-educated wife of a banker and mother of eighteen children, decided to make cheese in a small building at the corner of Mulberry and Grand in New York City. Today that cheese factory still exists and is presently run by Pina's grandson and her great-grandson, both named Robert Alleva.

Many things have changed since 1892 but, in Little Italy, many things have also remained the same. Just in front of the Alleva Latticini factory is a tiny retail store. Inside the shop one hears the banter of customers and owners who have known one another for years. This busy little store is the source of a constant flow of fresh and smoked Mozzarella, Ricotta, and aged cheeses, as well as fresh Italian cheese specialties. For four generations the residents of Manhattan have relied upon the high-quality fresh cheeses made in this small factory.

Originally, Alleva's customers were from the surrounding neighborhood but more recently people have come from all over the city, and even from other parts of the country. This may largely be a result of the recent demand for fresh, unadulterated food. These fresh foods have always been available and in fashion here at 188 Grand, in New York City. The demand for them has inspired others to make fresh Italian cheeses and New York City now boasts several dairies similar to Alleva.

Alleva Latticini has always been a family operation. In the beginning, Pina had the help of her brothers and could count on an occasional helping hand from her husband. When her husband died in 1908, she ran the business with some of her children. Living upstairs from the cheese plant, she was able to keep a keen eye on all the details. After World War II, Pina moved to Brooklyn but continued to travel into Manhattan every day on the bus until she was ninety-one. She must have truly loved her business. Like many cheese makers, she loved it because it was always a challenge. The milk never behaves precisely the same. She often said, "I have been in this business all my life and everyday I learn something new."

In the early days Alleva advertised on Italian radio, placed billboards on buses, and enjoyed considerable success. When the depression hit, it dealt a severe blow to this business as it did to many others. Alleva never regained its earlier success, though currently sales are healthy and growing. No longer advertising, Alleva manages, by word-of-mouth and a good reputation, to sell all the cheese it can produce. Most is sold in the retail store; the rest goes to local restaurants and to customers as far away as Seattle and California.

Alleva produces two types of cheese: Mozzarella and Ricotta. The curd for Mozzarella is produced by an affiliate cheese plant in upstate New York. Each week two thousand pounds of curd are shipped to the city cheese plant. The cheese maker at Alleva checks the curd for its ripeness. Robert Sr. likens the curd to a banana. When it is unripe and green, it is hard and must be allowed to ripen in a warm room. When it is ripe, it must be worked right away or stored in ice. To work it, he breaks up the curd, melts it, and then forms it into the various shapes: Mozzarella balls weighing eight or sixteen ounces, small egg-shaped Bocconcini, and Manteche, which consists of eight ounces of sweet butter surrounded by fresh Mozzarella. The Mozzarella balls may be left unsalted, briefly brined in salt, or smoked. The smoking is done "the old-fashioned way"—in a smoker for approximately ten minutes—rather than by soaking the cheese in a liquid smoke product.

Alleva's Ricotta (pronounced "rigut" by those in the business) is made entirely with whole milk. The milk is heated and vinegar or citric acid is added. The curd floats to the top, is skimmed off, and placed in perforated plastic molds, each holding one or three pounds of cheese. No salt is added so the cheese is sweet and extremely perishable. The Ricotta is made the old-fashioned way; the cheese is ladled directly from the vat into the molds, with a resultant uneven texture. In modern industrial plants, Ricotta is strained, homogenized, and extruded to fit perfectly into the containers that go to the consumer. At Alleva, one pound of Ricotta is determined by weight. The uneven texture will cause some of the cheese to sit above the top of the container, creating a truly handmade look for a delicious fresh cheese.

The elder Robert began his working life as a banker but the family business lured him back. Robert Jr. went to college and worked as a medical technician before becoming a cheese maker. The sense of family pride in this business has been evident for four generations. And throughout that time, the unique world that is Little Italy has remained largely unchanged. The sights, sounds, and smells of Italy abound. That air of ageless tradition continually draws members of the Alleva family back to the oldest *lateria* in America, started almost a hundred years ago by a most unusual immigrant woman.

Here a blend of typically Italian ingredients balances the flavors of sweet, salt, smoke, fruit, and spice.

2 red peppers, roasted, skinned, and halved
½ pound smoked Mozzarella, cut into four ½-inch-thick slices
4 or 8 anchovy fillets
Olive oil
Freshly ground black pepper
1 to 2 tablespoons chopped fresh parsley or basil
1 lemon, cut into 4 wedges

Arrange the red pepper halves on 4 plates. Place 1 slice of Mozzarella on each red pepper. Arrange 1 or 2 anchovy fillets atop the cheese. Drizzle with olive oil. Sprinkle with freshly ground black pepper and fresh parsley or basil. Serve at room temperature with lemon wedges.

Red, white, and green colors beckon the diner to this fresh, bright salad.

2 large garlic cloves, minced
2 tablespoons finely chopped parsley
¼ cup finely chopped fresh basil
⅔ cup olive oil
⅓ cup red wine vinegar
Salt and pepper to taste
4 Roma tomatoes, each cut into 12 pieces
6 Bocconcini (approximately ½ pound total)

Mix garlic, parsley, basil, oil, vinegar, salt, and pepper in a medium bowl. Add the tomatoes and Bocconcini. Toss lightly and marinate for at least 30 minutes before serving at room temperature.

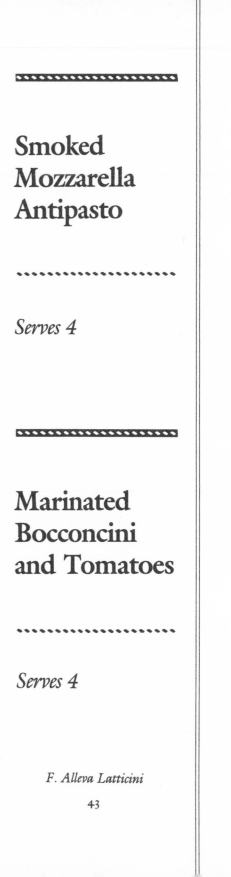

Smoked Mozzarella Antipasto

Serves 4

Marinated Bocconcini and Tomatoes

Serves 4

F. Alleva Latticini

Dennis's Mozzarella in Carrozza

Serves 1

Our friend, Dennis Calabi, fondly recollects rainy days on which he stayed home from school and relished this treat. These are the ingredients for one fried sandwich. Simply multiply for more.

1 slice (about 2 ounces) Mozzarella, ¼-inch thick
2 slices good quality white or French bread, crusts removed
1 or 2 anchovy fillets or ½ teaspoon anchovy paste
About 2 tablespoons milk
1 egg, beaten
½ cup bread crumbs
2 tablespoons oil, for frying

Trim the cheese so that it is half an inch smaller than the bread slices. Place the cheese and anchovies between the two pieces of bread. Moisten the outer edges of the bread with milk and press them together to seal. Dip the sandwich into the beaten egg and then into the bread crumbs. Heat oil in a medium skillet over medium heat. Fry in hot oil until brown and crisp on each side. Serve hot.

Gutsy red wine, crusty Italian bread, a warm summer evening, and this salad could make you believe that you have been transported to Italy.

2 red peppers, roasted, peeled, and seeded
2 yellow peppers, roasted, peeled, and seeded
2 large garlic cloves, minced
2/3 cup olive oil
1/4 cup sherry vinegar
2 tablespoons minced parsley
Salt and pepper to taste
1/4 cup oil-cured black or Niçoise olives, pitted and chopped
6 Bocconcini (approximately 1/2 pound total), each sliced into thirds

Slice the peppers into long, 1/4-inch-wide strips and cut them in half. In a medium bowl, mix the garlic, oil, vinegar, parsley, salt, and pepper. Add the pepper strips, olives, and Bocconcini. Toss lightly. Marinate for 30 minutes before serving at room temperature.

Marinated Bocconcini with Roasted Peppers

Serves 4

F. Alleva Latticini

Smoked Mozzarella and Eggs in Potato Baskets

Serves 2
as a main course

Eggs, smoked meat, and potatoes are standard breakfast partners. Here, smoked Mozzarella stands in for the meat and lightens this unusual brunch suggestion.

5 eggs
1 large unpeeled baking potato (approximately ½ pound), grated
1 teaspoon all-purpose flour
¼ teaspoon baking powder
¼ teaspoon black pepper
¼ teaspoon salt
3 tablespoons oil
1 tomato, peeled, seeded, and chopped
3 to 4 ounces smoked Mozzarella, grated or sliced
1 tablespoon minced fresh chives

Preheat the oven to 350°F. Mix one egg, the grated potato, flour, baking powder, pepper, and salt in a bowl. Heat the oil in a large skillet over medium heat. Pour the mixture into the hot skillet to form 4 pancakes. Turn when brown on the underside. Cook until the other side is brown, 4 to 5 minutes. Remove from skillet and, while they are still warm, mold into ½-cup ramekins or muffin tins to form a basket shape.

Bake the ramekins in the preheated oven for 10 to 15 minutes or until the potato baskets are slightly crunchy and will hold their shape. Remove the baskets from the oven. Distribute the chopped tomato and cheese among the potato baskets and return them to the oven.

Meanwhile, poach the remaining 4 eggs. The cheese will be melted when eggs are ready. Place 1 egg in each basket, sprinkle with minced chives, and serve immediately.

F. Alleva Latticini

Hand-ladling the curds into molds

Goat Folks

━◻━◻━◻━◻━◻━◻━◻━

*Interlaken
New York*

CHEESES: Goat cheese—
   Chabis, Crottin, Log,
   Pyramid, Tomme
RETAIL SALES: No
TOURS: No
MAIL ORDER: Yes

A seventy-seven-acre farm in the Finger Lakes region of New York has been the backdrop for two waves of city folk adopting a country life style and making goat cheese for an eager Manhattan market. The original characters in this script were Ian Zeiler and Denise Forant. The relative quiet of their upstate New York farm life followed years of more academic and cultured pursuits in Afghanistan, London, and Bordeaux. The present act features Kay and Howard Blume, transplants from a lively theatrical and artistic New York City milieu.

In Bordeaux Ian was completing his archeological studies. He and Denise tasted and relished the wine and food of the region and especially savored a local goat's milk cheese. Searching for its source, they discovered an ex-Parisian couple living on a small farm just outside Bordeaux. From them Denise learned to make cheese.

After three years in Bordeaux Denise, drawn back to the land, convinced Ian to move to America where they would make goat's milk cheese. They approached the new project systematically, writing numerous letters, inquiring about regulations for dairies and cheese manufacture. New York State appealed to them as a logical halfway point between Ian's family near New York City and Denise's in Canada. They planned to find and buy the land, prepare the cheese facility, and establish the venture. They would then be joined by two French friends and work as a foursome.

The property they purchased is not far from Cornell University, giving them access to the academic side of life. They became the first people in the area to practice organic farming on a large scale. That first year, in their innocence, they jumped into farming feet first, planting their sixty tillable acres to rye and buckwheat. At harvest time, they were duly astonished by the height and beauty of their full-grown crops: everything they knew about these crops they had garnered from books. They had never even seen the plants until they were growing in their own fields.

During that first year and a half, Denise drove the tractor while Ian built the cheese rooms and rebuilt the interior of the barn. Though it was no simple matter to find and procure the proper cheese-making equipment, they slowly accumulated what they needed.

As planned, their French friends arrived in October 1980. November and December proved to be arduous months marked by days filled with intense labor and nights with exhaustive discussion. By February their friends had returned to France. Left to themselves, Ian and Denise explored their alternatives. Should they abandon the undertaking? Was it too overwhelming for just the two of them? Denise was discouraged. But Ian, the eternal optimist, was entranced with his new life style and certain that they would succeed. He was determined to continue.

In the spring of 1981 they purchased their first two goats. That entire year was devoted to controlled and detailed experiments with the goats' milk: they would try something, try it another way, then try it again. By fall, they had developed their cheese and were selling it in the local markets.

By the following spring, their herd had expanded to twenty-five goats and the Ithaca market could no longer take all the cheese Ian was making. The next step was to branch out. But the five-hour journey to New York City would be a treacherous trip for their precious and fragile cheeses. To send his fresh cheeses from Ithaca to Manhattan in perfect condition, Ian invented a series of ingenious protective devices, using among other things, Igloo coolers, egg crates, PVC pipes, and chopsticks. He regaled us with amusing and painful stories of numerous shipping nightmares. But Ian clearly enjoyed the challenges of packaging and shipping and managed to solve the problems.

The farm continued to feed their herd of goats, which had increased to a hundred milkers. Fortunately for Ian, the popularity of his cheese increased in direct proportion to the increase in his milk supply. Eventually, they discontinued milking their own goats, which took up too much time, in favor of the efficiency of contracting with a local producer for their milk requirements.

Goat Folks' biggest seller is the Chabis, a very fresh, moist, and light goat cheese. Its whey drains for only one day, then the infant cheese is shipped to its destination. Perhaps this explains the extraordinary lengths to which Ian was willing to go to devise safe and secure shipping containers for his cheese. They also produce a Pyramid, coated with black pepper or herbs. This is considered a fresh cheese though it is aged slightly longer than is the Chabis and so acquires a more pronounced goat flavor. Ian has developed some aged cheeses. We particularly liked the four-month-old aged Tomme. This is a large cheese, weighing between three and five pounds, dense and intensely flavored, and encrusted with the natural molds that develop over the months. It requires a greater depth of knowledge and considerably more skill to age cheese in this manner than it does merely to produce a simple young cheese.

We asked him, "Where do you see yourself ten years from now?" Ian answered in a characteristically thoughtful manner: "I don't know what is going to happen in the future. I didn't expect to be where I am today five years ago."

Within a year, Ian and Denise had sold the farm and traveled to Thailand. The Blumes were the buyers. Kay Blume, disenchanted with life as an actress in films, the theater, and TV commercials, had enrolled in a New York restaurant school. There she tasted goat cheese and loved it at first bite. Her husband, Howard, had been working as a commercial film director, potter, writer, and graphic designer. After four years of searching for country property and a business close to a university, they found Goat Folks Farm.

Kay and Howard had carefully studied the market for goat cheese before they bought the business. They found it to be a growing one and decided to expand Ian's operation immediately. They built new curing and drying rooms, found a new milk supply, and are planning to produce some new cheeses. Ian taught them the basics and agreed to provide additional consultation as needed. Kay acknowledges that she is still a neophyte. Describing their first months as cheese makers, she said, "It was like taking the final when you haven't been to class!"

Nonetheless, the Blumes feel that they are finally home. They are fulfilled, energized, and content with their new vocation. Though Goat Folks Farm has changed hands, the original characters and the present players appear to be inspired by the same muse.

A special thank-you to Thomas J. McCombie, chef de cuisine at Chez TJ in Mountain View, California, for this delicious first course.

½ cup pink peppercorns
8 ounces fresh log-shaped Goat Cheese, cut into ½-inch rounds
1 cup all-purpose flour
2 eggs beaten with 2 tablespoons water
1 cup fine bread crumbs
3 cups port, preferably a vintage type
1 shallot, minced
⅔ cup sweet butter, softened
Salt and ground white pepper, to taste
2 quarts good cooking oil

Press a teaspoon or so of the pink peppercorns into each side of the cheese rounds. Dredge the rounds in flour, then in egg and, finally, in bread crumbs. Place in the refrigerator for at least one hour to firm. May be prepared a day ahead.

In a saucepan, cook the port and the minced shallot until the liquid is reduced to half a cup. Port is very flammable, so be careful. It should be very dark red, not burned, and have the body of a light syrup. Whisk in the softened butter and season with salt and pepper. Keep sauce warm.

In a deep fryer, heat the oil to 325°F. Drop in the cheese rounds. Cook until they are golden brown, about 2 minutes. Gently turn to cook on the other side. Remove the rounds from the oil and drain on paper towels. Divide the sauce among 8 serving plates. Place one round in center of each plate. Serve immediately.

Note: If you do not have a deep fryer, use a skillet: heat 1 inch of oil to 325°F and fry the cheese rounds until they are golden brown. Carefully flip and continue to cook. Using this method, you will have to fry the cheese in batches. Work quickly so that the first batch will still be hot when served.

French-Fried Goat Cheese with Port and Pink Peppercorns

Serves 8

Goat Folks

Black Bean Soup with Pumpkin and Chèvre Purée

Serves 8

Sweet, spicy, and substantial, this soup sports the traditional Halloween colors. It is a natural for the fall when pumpkins are plentiful, but easy to make all year round.

1 cup dried black beans, soaked in water overnight
6 cups water
1 bay leaf
1 teaspoon black mustard seeds
1 teaspoon cumin seeds
1 large carrot, finely chopped
1 large celery stalk, finely chopped
1 medium onion, finely chopped
4 tablespoons butter
1 teaspoon coriander seeds, crushed
¼ teaspoon ground cayenne pepper
1 teaspoon salt
½ teaspoon black pepper
2 or 3 tablespoons chopped chives and/or cilantro

Cook the black beans in water until tender, 1½ to 2 hours. Meanwhile, sauté the bay leaf, mustard and cumin seeds, carrot, celery, and onion in butter for 20 to 30 minutes until the vegetables are soft and lightly browned. Add the mixture to the cooked beans. Add the coriander seeds, cayenne, salt, and pepper. Remove the bay leaf and purée the mixture in a blender or food processor. Return to the pot and add extra water to thin, if necessary. Adjust seasoning.

Pumpkin and Chèvre Purée
4 garlic cloves, chopped
1 tablespoon butter
1 cup pumpkin purée, fresh or canned
2 ounces fresh Goat Cheese
½ teaspoon orange zest
¼ teaspoon salt

Sauté the garlic in butter until soft. Add the pumpkin and heat through. Add the Goat Cheese, orange zest, and salt. Thin with water if necessary. Heat gently and quickly so that the cheese does not curdle.

Pour hot bean soup into bowls, top with a dollop of Pumpkin and Chèvre Purée, sprinkle with chopped chives, and serve.

Excellent apéritif fare, these turnovers are plump with Goat Cheese and some of its favorite partners.

   1 sheet frozen puff pastry, thawed
   1 red bell pepper, roasted, peeled, seeded, and chopped
   5 ounces fresh Goat Cheese
   1 tablespoon olive oil
   1 small head roasted garlic, cloves separated and peeled (recipe
      follows)

Roll puff pastry to a thickness of ¼ inch. Cut into 3-inch squares. Combine the pepper, goat cheese, olive oil, and garlic cloves. Place a tablespoon of the mixture in the center of each square. Fold the pastry corner to corner to make triangles. Seal the edges with water, pinching tightly. Bake on a cookie sheet in a 400°F oven for 8 to 10 minutes until puffed and browned. Serve hot.

Roasted Garlic
Preheat the oven to 350°F. Remove the outer paper-thin skin from a head of garlic, but do not peel or break apart the cloves. Carefully slice off the tips of the cloves without detaching them. Place in small pan and sprinkle with olive oil. Bake uncovered for about 30 to 40 minutes, until the garlic is soft.

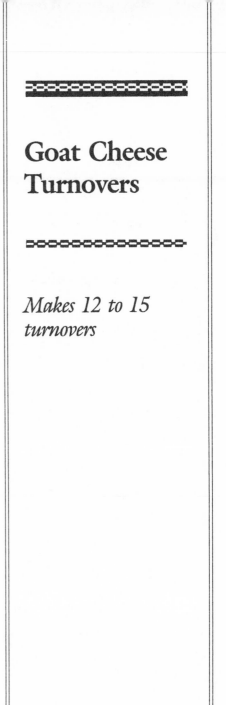

Goat Cheese Turnovers

Makes 12 to 15 turnovers

Smoked Salmon and Chèvre Pasta

*Serves 4
as a first course*

Bright and colorful, this rich pasta just might steal the show. If you are adventurous, try it for breakfast one day.

10 ounces dried, or 1 pound fresh, fettuccine
2 tablespoons butter
½ cup green onions, chopped
2 teaspoons capers
1 teaspoon lemon zest
½ cup heavy cream
Freshly ground black pepper
4 ounces fresh Goat Cheese
12 cherry tomatoes, halved
2 ounces mild smoked salmon, chopped

Cook the pasta al dente.

Meanwhile, melt the butter in a skillet. Add the green onions, capers, lemon zest, and cream. Simmer until slightly thickened. Add a generous quantity of black pepper and 2 ounces of the Goat Cheese. Stir over low heat until the cheese melts.

Just before serving, add the tomatoes and salmon. Cook until just heated. Drain the pasta and place on a serving dish. Crumble the remaining cheese over the pasta, top with sauce, and toss. Serve immediately.

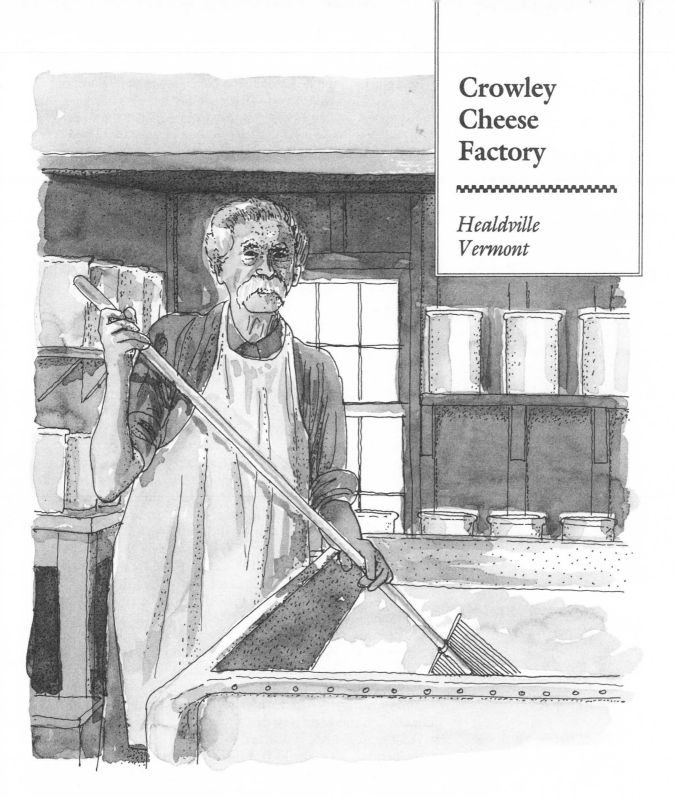

Cutting the curds with a cheese harp

Crowley Cheese Factory

....

Healdville Vermont

CHEESE: Crowley
Colby—Mild, Sharp,
and flavored with
Garlic, Hot Pepper,
Caraway, or Dill
RETAIL SALES: Yes
TOURS: Yes
MAIL ORDER: Yes

A light fog muted the dramatic fall colors as we wound our way up Healdville Road. That early fall morning we were to visit the Crowley Cheese Factory in Healdville, Vermont. The factory is housed in a picturesque century-old wood frame building and the small adjacent parking lot seems barely large enough to accommodate the eight tour buses that are expected each day.

Vermont's oldest cheese factory was built in 1882 by Winfield and Nellie Crowley. The Crowley family's practice of making cheese for neighbors in the farm kitchen became a business when Winfield opened a formal cheese factory. It was operated through the years by the Crowley family until Winfield's grandson, Robert, died suddenly of a heart attack.

Randolph Smith and his wife had recently retired to their summer home not far from the Crowley factory. Randolph had known Robert and his father, George, and had always admired the cheese factory and its place in Vermont's history. Wryly describing his entry into the cheese business, Randolph Smith quipped, "I made a mistake and started asking questions. Next thing I knew, I had retired into the cheese business. Appropriately enough, I became the owner of the cheese factory on April Fool's Day of 1967."

It is obvious, however, that Randolph Smith was no fool. He had devoted his working life to education. His first teaching post was at the American University in Beirut. Eventually, he returned to America to continue his education and acquire more degrees. During the last twenty-five years before he retired, he had served as director of a respected private school in New York. He was attracted by the Crowley Cheese Factory not because of an avid love of the cheese business nor from any particular affection for cheese, but because he wanted to save a piece of history. He remarked, "The past goes by pretty fast these days and, unless we hold on to a little bit of it, people won't know how it used to be."

A visit to the Crowley Cheese Factory certainly provides a living example of how it used to be. The Colby cheese is made entirely by hand with the original wooden presses and tables, in the same way that it was made in 1882 when Winfield started. Milk is warmed to seventy degrees, a sour milk culture is added, the heat is increased to ninety degrees, and the culture is allowed to grow for approximately ninety minutes. Rennet is added and, after forty-five minutes, the curd is cut. As part of the Colby process, the curd is baled out of the whey, rinsed with cool spring water, and then broken up in small bits and worked for half an hour. Rinsing off the acidic whey produces a milder, sweeter cheese than Colby. Colby also differs from Cheddar in that its curds are not "milled," so Colby is moister and more loosely packed; Cheddar has no holes and is drier and harder in texture.

After the curd is rinsed and worked by hand, salt is added at a rate of four ounces of salt for every ten pounds of unpressed cheese curd. The curds are transferred to 2½-, 5-, and 25-pound molds and then pressed in hand-cranked presses. When the cheese wheels have formed, they are placed in the curing room for three or four days and then dipped in wax. Crowley's mild cheese is aged for two months; the sharp for six months.

Crowley Colby is exceedingly popular and deservedly so. Here is a perfect example of a delicious and well-flavored cheese that is not overly strong or acidic. Thousands of visitors from all over the world tour the factory each year. Prominently displayed in the main room of the factory is a world map dotted with blue pins to represent places from which visitors have come and red pins to represent places to which cheese has been shipped. The map is a sea of blue and red.

Every visitor gains some knowledge of and appreciation for the way good old-fashioned cheese is made. The visitors leave with a taste for Crowley Colby and, generally, with plans to order more in the future. These guests are the basis of a large mailing list from which a great percentage of Crowley's cheese is sold. Even retail outlets order directly from the plant. Christmas orders are so numerous that the plant must stop production during November and December so that the mail orders can be processed.

Although Randolph Smith spoke as though he simply fell into the cheese business, he has found it rewarding and quite suitable to his nature. His commitment to preserving part of Vermont's history and his enthusiasm for meeting people found an appropriate outlet here. He was also very pleased that his two sons, Peter and Kent, found the business interesting. By the time Randolph died, in 1987, Peter had already assumed the major responsibilities of management and was in a position to continue the operation in his father's stead. And another family tradition has begun.

Crowley Cheese Factory

Healdville Mushroom Salad

Serves 4

½ pound fresh mushrooms, washed, dried, and thinly sliced
¼ pound Colby, thinly sliced to match the size of the mushrooms
⅓ cup finely chopped parsley
¼ cup fresh lemon juice (about 1½ lemons)
¼ cup olive oil
½ teaspoon salt
½ teaspoon ground black pepper
¼ teaspoon ground cayenne pepper
Small bunch green-leaf lettuce
1 ounce fresh *enoki* mushrooms (optional)

Combine the fresh mushrooms, cheese, and parsley in a small mixing bowl. Mix the lemon juice, oil, salt, black pepper, and cayenne in a separate bowl. Toss the mushrooms with the lemon juice mixture.

Line a serving bowl or plate with the leaf lettuce and mound the mushroom salad. Decoratively arrange the *enoki* mushrooms on top and serve.

Posted on a wall at the Crowley Cheese Factory was a weathered newspaper clipping that inspired this recipe.

Half a loaf French bread, crusts removed, and cut into 1-inch slices
Dijon mustard
½ pound Colby, grated (2 cups)
4 eggs
2 cups (or more) milk

Spread mustard lightly on one side of each slice of bread. Arrange half the bread slices on the bottom of a buttered 8-cup soufflé dish. Cover the bread with half of the cheese. Layer with the remaining bread slices and top with the remaining cheese.

Mix the eggs and milk and pour over the bread layers. The liquid should almost reach the top of the dish; add more milk if necessary.

Bake in a 350°F oven for 25 to 30 minutes, until the soufflé balloons and is lightly browned on top. Serve immediately.

Poor Man's Soufflé

Serves 4 to 6

Crowley Cheese Factory

Fried Wontons

Makes 15 or 16 wontons

You will find it impossible to make enough of these palate-pleasers. Serve them as an appetizer or as cocktail fare. The filling can easily be mixed in a food processor. Grate the cheese with the processor, then add the other ingredients, and process until just blended.

2 ounces fresh oyster or *shiitake* mushrooms, chopped
2 tablespoons olive oil
4 ounces grated Colby (1 cup)
2 green onions, chopped (½ cup)
1 teaspoon minced fresh ginger
1 handful chopped cilantro leaves
½ teaspoon Szechwan peppercorns, crushed
15 or 16 wonton skins
Vegetable oil
Hot Chinese mustard or chili sauce

Sauté the mushrooms in olive oil until slightly browned. Combine the mushrooms with the cheese, green onions, ginger, cilantro, and peppercorns in a small mixing bowl.

Fill each wonton skin by placing approximately 1 heaping teaspoon of the mushroom mixture in the center of each square. Moisten the edges with water and fold into a triangle. Pinch the long ends together, sealing with water.

In a large cast-iron skillet or deep fryer, heat at least 2 inches of oil. The oil is ready when a wonton skin sizzles when dropped into it. Drop 4 or 5 wontons at a time into the hot oil. The skins will swell almost immediately and begin to turn brown. Flip them over and remove from the oil when all sides are browned. Drain on paper towels. Repeat with the remaining wontons. Serve immediately with Chinese mustard or chili sauce.

Shelburne Farms

....

*Shelburne
Vermont*

Shelburne Farms

....

*Shelburne
Vermont*

CHEESES: Cheddar—
  Medium, Sharp, and
  Extra Sharp
RETAIL SALES: Yes
TOURS: Yes, June–
  September
MAIL ORDER: Yes

On the eastern shore of Lake Champlain lies a grand estate built on proceeds from America's early industrial era. Today the meticulously tended grounds, one-hundred-room mansion, and glorious barns and other buildings house the Shelburne Farms nonprofit land trust and cheese factory.

The general manager is Alec Webb, a grandson of William Webb who originally commissioned the building of this estate. Marrying into the Vanderbilt family, William Webb acquired the resources to indulge his interest in hackney horses. The barn, one of the largest in the country, was originally built to house his prize-winning horses and his sheep and cows.

The glory days of this lovely estate, built in 1886, lasted only into the 1920s. What with wars, deaths, and income taxes the Webbs could not continue to maintain its grandeur. In the early 1950s Alec's father turned the estate into a working farm. After studying at Cornell, he began raising hardy Brown Swiss cows, a breed he felt was especially suited to the harsh Vermont climate.

Alec's generation inherited the problem of the future of their farm. It was for them to decide whether to divide the property among the heirs or to find some way to keep it intact. Their novel solution was to turn the property into an agricultural trust and nonprofit organization. This form of ownership allows the property to remain intact, to be refurbished, to flourish, and to permit the public access to all its splendor. The property is no longer owned by the Webbs themselves and is operated by a Board of Directors. The Board hired Alec Webb to be the general manager. Alec's brother, Marshall, who is on the Board of Directors, manages the buildings, grounds, and woodlands.

When today's generation of Webbs assumed control of Shelburne Farms, the milk produced by the Brown Swiss herd was sold on the wholesale market. In an effort to increase revenue, it was decided to sell raw milk under Shelburne's own label. Because there is only a limited market for raw milk, the Board decided to process the milk into cheese—a product with wider appeal and more versatility. Rather than produce some esoteric fresh or ripening cheese, the Webbs chose to honor their Vermont roots and make a high-quality hand-made Cheddar.

Bill Clapp was bottling raw milk for the farm when the decision was made to switch to cheese. Bill had worked in the food business for many years, in restaurants as well as in food production. He applauded the decision and proceeded to teach himself to make cheese, garnering information in factories in Canada and on the East Coast and from consultants and cheese makers brought to the farm. Piece by piece, Bill Clapp acquired the art of creating delicious Cheddar in small batches.

We visited Bill in the tiny production room while he "cheddared" the large slabs of cheese curd. To the background music of cheese slapping on cheese and stainless steel, he described his process. Five days a week Bill fills the five-hundred-gallon vat with four thousand pounds of milk. He heats it, adds culture, and then cuts and stirs the curd. Next, he drains the whey and allows the curds to settle, forming a large, glossy mat. When the proper acidity has developed, he and his assistant heft the heavy curd mats into a milling machine that cuts the curds into small squares. This process of allowing the curds to form mats and then cutting them into squares separates a true Cheddar from Colby or other stirred-curd aged cheeses.

After the curds are cut, they are salted and transferred to large steel hoops. The filled hoops are pressed for several hours and then the forty-pound blocks of cheese are wrapped in foil and set to age. Shelburne Farms markets three types of cheese, medium, sharp, and extra sharp. All the cheese is aged for a minimum of six months; the extra sharp for at least two years. The end product is a toothsome white Cheddar of unusually fine texture and complex, rich flavor. Half of all their production is sold directly to the consumer either at the Farm or by mail order. The rest is sold directly to specialty cheese shops throughout the country, though primarily in New England and New York.

Working for Shelburne Farms is rewarding for Bill Clapp. "Money's great! I get to be my own boss. I get to live on the lake right next to that one-hundred-room mansion, in this beautiful location. But, by the same token, I am always here. In case someone doesn't come into work, I get the call." He feels blessed by the quality of Shelburne's Brown Swiss milk and believes that its solids-to-fat ratio is the best possible for making Cheddar. Most cheese makers he has met complain of a constant battle for consistent milk quality. Bill covets the first prize in one of the big cheese competitions held in Wisconsin and believes he has a good chance. "Small cheese makers can turn out a better cheese if they want to. If you stir that stuff by hand all day long, it keeps you honest. In the big places, all the cheese maker can do is push a button. I figure if I am going to spend eight to ten hours a day doing this and I am well paid, the least I can do is put out the best product I can."

Life at Shelburne Farms today retains much of the elegance it had one hundred years ago. The beautiful grounds and buildings gracefully host summer concerts; there are nature walking trails for Institute members and a program for conservation education. The mammoth barn houses cheese aging rooms, a bakery, and a furniture-making shop. A visitors' center and the farm store are situated near the entrance to the property. Renovation of the family mansion has transformed it into a country inn with an excellent restaurant serving local food products, including Shelburne Farmhouse Cheddar. The Webbs hope that all these ventures will give new life to their family home while providing a market for Shelburne's products and those of surrounding farmstead producers.

We thank Michael Clark, of La Selva Beach, California, for this rich and savory soup that is quickly put together.

½ cup butter
1 medium yellow onion, diced
½ cup all-purpose flour
6 cups milk
1 bunch broccoli, chopped
1 teaspoon cayenne pepper
1 tablespoon Dijon mustard
½ cup beer
1 cup half-and-half or light cream
1 teaspoon Worcestershire sauce
1 pound Cheddar, grated (4 cups)
Salt and pepper

In a large pot, melt the butter over medium heat. Add the onion and cook gently until soft. Lower the heat and add the flour. Cook gently, stirring, for 3 to 4 minutes. Do not allow to brown. Slowly add the milk, stirring constantly until the mixture is smooth and begins to thicken. Add the broccoli, cayenne, mustard, and beer. Simmer until the broccoli softens, approximately 5 to 8 minutes. Add the half-and-half and the Worcestershire sauce. Simmer for 3 to 5 minutes until the broccoli is tender. Add the cheese, stirring until it has melted. Add salt and pepper to taste.

Broccoli and Cheese Soup

Serves 6 to 8

Cheddar-Dressed Arugula Salad

Serves 4

If you thought the last recipe was quick and easy, try this. Arugula is definitely our favorite salad green. We grow it in our gardens because it is not always readily available. An acceptable substitute would be watercress or a combination of watercress and spinach.

4 ounces Cheddar, grated (1 cup)
3½ tablespoons raspberry vinegar
5 tablespoons walnut oil
½ teaspoon freshly ground black pepper
4 to 6 handfuls arugula leaves

Mix gently in a small bowl the cheese, vinegar, oil, and pepper. Wash and dry the arugula. Toss the cheese dressing with the arugula and serve immediately.

These individually filled chiles are best cooked on a charcoal grill, but you may use a very hot oven or a broiler. They are a lively accompaniment to any simply grilled meat or fish.

6 fresh Anaheim chiles
2 tablespoons olive oil
1 or 2 garlic cloves, minced
½ teaspoon ground cumin
1½ cups corn kernels (2 large ears if using fresh)
¼ teaspoon salt
6 ounces sharp Cheddar, grated (1½ cups)

Lightly roast the chiles on a grill or under a broiler until they are slightly softened but not limp. Cool and slice open lengthwise, taking care not to cut through both sides and to leave the stem intact. Remove the seeds.

Heat the oil in a medium skillet. Add the garlic and cumin. Sauté until the garlic is soft. Add the corn. Cook gently for 3 to 5 minutes. Salt lightly and allow to cool. Add the cheese to the corn mixture and stuff it into the open chile pockets.

Just before serving, place the stuffed chiles on a hot grill, in a hot oven, or under the broiler until they are heated through and the cheese is melted, 3 to 4 minutes.

Corn and Cheddar-Stuffed Chiles

Serves 6

Shelburne Farms

Cheddar and Prune Muffins

Makes 14 to 18 muffins

Afternoon tea is presently enjoying a resurgence of popularity. We love these sweet and savory treats at any time of day and find them particularly pleasing with tea.

¾ cups boiling water
1½ cups pitted prunes, chopped (6 to 8 ounces)
2 tablespoons butter
2 cups all-purpose flour
¼ cup sugar
1 teaspoon baking powder
1 teaspoon baking soda
2 eggs, beaten
½ cup milk
¼ cup molasses
8 ounces Cheddar, coarsely grated (2 cups)
½ cup whole almonds, chopped (2 ounces)

In a small mixing bowl, pour boiling water over the prunes and butter. Cool.

Sift together the flour, sugar, baking powder, and soda.

In a separate bowl, mix together the eggs, milk, and molasses. Add the Cheddar and almonds to the dry ingredients. Add the prune mixture to the wet ingredients. Quickly combine the wet and dry ingredients until just mixed.

Fill buttered muffin tins two-thirds full and bake for 20 minutes at 350°F. To accentuate the Cheddar flavor, cool the muffins before serving them.

Guilford
Cheese
Company

*Guilford
Vermont*

Guilford Cheese Company

━━━━━━━━━━━━━━

Guilford
Vermont

CHEESES: Verde-Mont
    (Plain and Herb),
    Crème Fraîche, Mont-
    Bert, and Mont-Brie
RETAIL SALES: Yes; call
    first
TOURS: By appointment
MAIL ORDER: Yes

Late one autumn afternoon we arrived at Guilford Cheese Company in southern Vermont. No sooner had we turned off our car motor than the thick door of the unpainted clapboard house burst open and Ann Dixon emerged, all smiles and energy. Close on her heels skipped Amanda, her young daughter, followed by an assortment of cats and dogs. Ann suggested that as it would soon be dark, we must waste no time and meet her husband, John, who would take us on a tour of the barn. John appeared, smiling and gracious. The barn was built in 1975 for sheep, back when Ann was teaching and John, as now, was a surgeon at nearby Brattleboro Memorial Hospital. For as long as they could remember, they had entertained the notion of farming their land; this barn became the nucleus for that endeavor.

Eventually, the sheep were exchanged for a pair of steers to clear the land, a task that is now performed by a pair of giant Percheron horses. Then the Dixons decided to try their hands at milking a small herd of Jersey cows. Ann's romantic notion of delivering raw Jersey milk in the area soon became a bothersome chore so they elected to sell the rich milk in bulk to a co-op. But Ann missed the involvement with her product and John felt that their milk should fetch a higher price. How could they create some added value?

The answer for them was to make cheese, so Ann learned the basics of cheese making. She chose to make an original variety of cheese in an appealing, simple style not used elsewhere in Vermont. Thus was Verde-Mont created. It is a fresh, low-salt, farmstead cheese, quite unlike the Cheddar for which Vermont is famous. (A farmstead cheese is one produced on a farm from the milk of that farm's own animals.) The Dixons feel that this cheese is appropriate for Vermont, the home of Yankee ingenuity and independent thinkers.

Our tour provided a peek at the cheese room, attached to the barn and adjacent to the milk room. The Verde-Mont cheese-making process begins when milk is pumped from the bulk tank to the three-hundred-gallon vat pasteurizer dominating the tiny cheese room. There the milk is pasteurized and allowed to cool. A culture is added and the acidity allowed to develop.

Once the cream has risen and thickened, it is skimmed off and used for crème fraîche. The next day, if the curd has developed enough acid, it is scooped into bags that are hung from hooks and allowed to drain. The cheese is then seasoned, shaped in plastic molds, and aged under refrigeration for three days. The taste is bland, clean, and uncomplicated—somewhat like a Farmer's Cheese or a dry, small-curd Cottage Cheese, or a dry, tight Ricotta. The Dixons offer either a plain or herbed version of Verde-Mont, packaged by hand in an appealing and sophisticated wrap that they designed themselves.

That evening we were introduced to their sons, Peter and Sam, the other two principals in the Guilford Cheese Company. Sam is the herdsman and farm manager, an occupation for which he prepared by graduating from the University of Vermont with a degree in animal science. The official Guilford cheese maker is Peter, who learned his craft from Ann. He is an avid experimenter and has produced fresh cheese mixed with apricots, fresh cheese layered in a torte with basil and pine nuts, and a version of Camembert.

Dinner ready, we gathered around a large antique table in a cozy dining room lit entirely by candles. While we ate a hearty New England dinner, a family discussion of dreams, plans, and philosophy was our food for thought. The Dixons have found a way to provide for themselves and to fulfill each individual's particular needs while preserving the family unit.

John spoke of the family cheese company as his retirement project, so strongly did he believe in its success. He was, in fact, investing his income in the potential of their fledgling family enterprise. They were all wondering whether they could sell enough cheese to support themselves. They wanted to expand their tiny operation to its limits, but they did not know if, even then, it could generate enough income for three families. With a twinkle in his eye, John suggested that they develop their business to its maximum, sell out, and start all over again. The family response to his half-serious proposal was a resounding dissent. Peter, so content with his work, had no interest in giving it up. Sam protested that he wished to be able to pass the business to the younger generation that would eventually emerge. John looked pleased, and we speculated that he frequently played devil's advocate in order to measure the degree of commitment and energy his sons might possess at any given moment. Once the commotion had subsided, John stated, in a more serious vein, that marketing is the key. The family agreed that almost anyone can produce cheese, but not everyone can sell it.

Selling the cheese is Ann's task. She participates in at least one food-oriented event every month. So enamored is she of their products that she eagerly discusses them with anyone who is interested. Responsibility for the distribution of their product means time spent on marketing projects and frequent trips to Boston. Part of her marketing efforts for Guilford Cheese is her connection with Vermont Specialty Food Producers, a marketing organization for the growing and diverse specialty products of Vermont.

Ann's participation in this group is most appropriate since she and John feel a strong connection to Vermont. Their affinity stretches beyond their own 125-acre farm to include the larger community of specialty food producers in their state. They identify with others who follow their dreams by creating products that reflect life in Vermont.

The next morning we said our good-byes. As we drove away, we reflected upon the future of this type of farmstead endeavor. It is inherently a part of this country's past, but we wonder if it can survive in the future. In this case at least, we felt that it could. So forceful is the Dixon family spirit and drive that their success seems guaranteed.

In mid-1987, the Dixons had expanded their business and, through an arrangement with the French cheese company, Fromagerie Renard-Gillard, they hired two consultants to guide them in the manufacture of French-style Brie and Camembert. They erected a large, new cheese factory on their farm and now make Mont-Bert, a type of Camembert, and Mont-Brie, a type of Brie. The new facility requires more milk than they could produce on their farm, so they sold their cows and now buy all their milk from neighboring farms. With this reorganization came the realization that they could not do it by themselves; they lacked the necessary financial and managerial abilities. Fortunately, they acquired some innovative investors and have a distribution arrangement with Cabot Farmers' Co-op.

Radicchio is a red-leaf, bitter lettuce of Italian origin recently available in American markets. If you are unable to find it, sharp and spicy mustard greens may be substituted. Although this dish is best grilled over charcoal, you can also use a broiler.

  12 ounces Camembert, rind removed, cut into 12 pieces
  12 large radicchio leaves, blanched and patted dry
  ¼ cup balsamic vinegar
  ½ cup fruity olive oil
  Salt and pepper to taste

Place 1 piece of cheese in the middle of each radicchio leaf. Wrap the cheese in the leaf and close with a toothpick.

  Mix together the vinegar, olive oil, salt, and pepper. Brush the cheese packages lightly with the oil and vinegar mixture.

  Place the packages on a hot grill. Turn after approximately 2 minutes. The radicchio should be soft and browned but not burned. Remove from the fire and place on individual serving plates. Drizzle the packages with the remaining vinaigrette and serve warm.

Grilled Stuffed Radicchio

Serves 6

Guilford Cheese Company

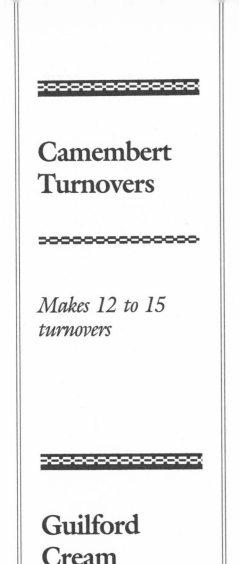

Camembert Turnovers

Makes 12 to 15 turnovers

Camembert, apples, and Calvados, an apple brandy, are plentiful in the Normandy region of France. Indigenous to Vermont are apples, applejack, and, now, Guilford Cheese Company's version of Camembert.

6 ounces Camembert, rind removed
1 apple, peeled, cored, and minced
2 tablespoons Calvados or applejack
⅛ teaspoon mace
1 sheet frozen puff pastry, thawed

Mix the Camembert, apple, Calvados, and mace.

Roll out the puff pastry to a thickness of ¼ inch and cut into 3-inch squares. Place a tablespoon of the cheese mixture in the middle of each square and fold it corner-to-corner to make a triangle. Seal the edges with water, pinching tightly.

Bake on a cookie sheet in a 400°F oven for 8 to 10 minutes, until puffed and browned. Serve hot.

Guilford Cream

Serves 6 to 8

This is our adaptation of a dessert recipe from Ann Dixon.

1 packet unflavored gelatin
½ cup boiling water
2 Plain Verde-Mont cheeses (5¼ ounces each)
½ cup milk, cream, or crème fraîche
3 tablespoons maple syrup
1 teaspoon fresh lemon juice

Dissolve the gelatin in the boiling water.

Blend the cheese, milk, maple syrup, and lemon juice until the mixture is the consistency of sour cream. Gently combine the cheese mixture with the gelatin. Pour into a mold and chill.

Serve plain or with a fruit purée or melted and thinned raspberry jam.

After the sandwiches are assembled, the remaining halves of the red and yellow peppers might serve as a crisp and colorful garnish for this novel lunch fare. To complete the meal, offer a consommé or a green salad.

6 slices French bread, each 1 inch thick
Olive oil
2 tablespoons butter
½ pound fresh *shiitake* mushrooms, thickly sliced
1 small red onion, coarsely chopped
Half a red pepper, cut lengthwise in strips, then crosswise in half
Half a yellow pepper, cut lengthwise in strips, then crosswise in half
Generous amount of ground black pepper
½ teaspoon dried tarragon
2 tablespoons cognac
6 ounces Camembert, rind removed, cut into 6 equal portions

Brush the bread slices lightly with olive oil on both sides and toast them.

Melt the butter in a sauté pan, add the mushrooms, onion, and peppers, and sauté until softened. Add the black pepper and tarragon, stirring lightly. Sprinkle with cognac.

Spoon the mushroom mixture onto the toasts. Top with cheese and place under the broiler until the cheese is just melted. Serve immediately.

Open-faced Camembert Sandwiches

Makes 6 sandwiches

Guilford Cheese Company

Verde-Mont Bread Pudding

Serves 8

Here is a comforting, satisfying dessert that is just as suitable for breakfast. We like it served warm (and often!), as it is, or with maple syrup or a fruit purée.

Half a loaf French bread, crust removed and reserved, cut into 1-inch cubes
1½ cups milk
2 tablespoons bourbon whiskey
3 tablespoons butter
2 eggs
¾ cup plus 2 tablespoons sugar
¾ teaspoon cinnamon
½ teaspoon pure vanilla extract
¼ teaspoon nutmeg
2 teaspoons grated orange zest
5 ounces Verde-Mont, loosely crumbled

Preheat the oven to 350°F. Soak the bread cubes in the milk and bourbon.

In a food processor or blender, crumble the bread crusts, which will yield about 2 cups.

Butter a 1-quart soufflé dish, of any shape, with 1 tablespoon of the butter and dust with some bread crumbs.

Mix together the eggs, ¾ cup of the sugar, ½ teaspoon of the cinnamon, the vanilla, nutmeg, and orange zest. Combine this mixture with the bread cubes and gently fold in the crumbled cheese. Pour into the soufflé dish.

Melt the remaining 2 tablespoons butter and mix with ¾ cup of the crust crumbs, ¼ teaspoon cinnamon, and 2 tablespoons sugar. Top the pudding with the crumb mixture and bake in the preheated oven for 35 to 40 minutes, until puffy and lightly browned.

Cabot
Farmers'
Co-op

Cabot
Vermont

Cabot Farmers' Co-op

▄▄▄▄▄▄▄▄▄▄▄▄▄▄▄▄▄▄▄

Cabot
Vermont

CHEESES: Cheddar—
Mild, Sharp, Extra
Sharp, Hunter's Extra
Sharp, and Private
Stock (which is two
years old), Monterey
Jack, Brick, Cottage,
and Cold-Pack Cheese
RETAIL SALES: Yes
TOURS: By appointment
MAIL ORDER: Yes

The largest and one of the oldest commercial producers of Cheddar in Vermont has survived and flourished for almost seventy years. Perhaps this is because the Cabot Farmers' Co-op reflects the rugged and sturdy character of the land and people of the surrounding area. Or perhaps Cabot's survival is due to the exceptionally high-quality Cheddar produced. Recollections of its rich, complex flavor, smooth texture, and lack of bitterness accompanied us as we approached the tiny community of Cabot.

The enchanting country road must be too small, we thought, for the giant milk tanker trucks so necessary for a booming cheese plant. But then we arrived and pulled in behind some of those same trucks. Awaiting us at the Cabot Co-op was Alan Parker, coordinator of marketing and sales. A native Vermonter and veteran of many aspects of the dairy business, Alan was to provide us with considerable insight into Cabot Cheddar, local agriculture, and the Vermont spirit.

Until the early 1900s Vermont, like much of the rest of the country, had an agrarian economy. Most people lived an almost self-sufficient existence on small farms. On each farm there were a few cows, from whose milk cheese was made. Eventually, as milk production increased, each small community built its own creamery to process the excess local milk into butter. The butter was sold in Boston; the skimmed milk and buttermilk given back to the farms for feed or simply discarded.

As the modern world brought with it centralization and specialization, one after another the small creameries folded. In Cabot, ninety stubborn local farmers contributed five dollars for each cow they owned, bought the local creamery, and established their own cooperative. The total investment represented only eight hundred cows but it kept the endeavour alive. They continued to produce and sell butter until the cost of producing milk made it impractical to ignore the skimmed milk and the buttermilk. In the 1930s a master cheese maker was hired and Cabot Co-op began making Cheddar.

In Vermont, one of our smallest and least populated states, no business is very large. Cabot, however, has thrived. Presently it processes 300 million pounds of milk each year from five hundred farms. We asked why this large creamery survived when others did not. Alan Parker answered that

Cabot's early management was more "forward looking" than that of other co-ops and that the progressive management continues today. Cabot's plant manager and the Board of Directors (which consists of thirteen farmers) know that a good product is of little value unless you can sell it. They are keenly interested in the consumer and this is reflected in the thrust of their marketing efforts.

The focus of Cabot's marketing is increased name recognition for fluid milk, butter, yogurt, cottage cheese, and premium Cheddar. A growing consumer interest in specialty cheeses has spurred production of one- and three-pound Cheddars, waxed and attractively packaged. Alan explained, "Few people would give as a gift a wedge of Cheddar wrapped in plastic, but a beautifully waxed and labeled cheese is another story."

Dairymen everywhere believe that their particular farming conditions produce the best quality milk. Alan, no exception, readily launched into his theory. In Great Britain, where Cheddar originated, it is believed that the best cheeses are made from milk produced by cows raised on hillside farms. The hills of northern Vermont, where hay grows well, support the Cabot herds. The bulk of their diet is supplied by roughage from dry hay rather than by corn silage, a common component of cows' diets elsewhere in the country. Alan assured us that cows prefer hay. Seeking to substantiate his contention, we learned that no cows were available for interview that day.

Because they produce large quantities of milk, Holstein-Friesian cows are found on most dairy farms in this country. Other breeds, such as Jersey, Ayrshire, and Guernsey, yield less milk but what they give is generally richer in butterfat and protein. Richer milk produces a higher yield of cheese for each pound of milk. Cabot's policy of paying a premium for higher solids (protein) as well as butterfat, encourages local farmers to raise those breeds with a richer yield. A high yield of cheese from a given amount of milk is crucial to cheese producers, especially those making Cheddar. That extra measure of cheese for each dollar spent on milk becomes more important each month the cheese ages. The aging of cheese requires additional capital expenditures for facilities, refrigeration, and handling. For the Cheddar producer, a considerable amount of money is tied up in the raw product for the six to twenty-four months that the cheese rests, garnering flavor but not profits. It is estimated that each pound of cheese costs the producer two cents per month in interest alone. Time and time again we visited cheese facilities at which Cheddar has been replaced by Mozzarella, String Cheese, or Jack. For many small cheese factories throughout the country it has become a matter of survival to manufacture a cheese that can be processed, wrapped, and shipped almost the same day. At Cabot Co-op a Monterey Jack is made primarily to keep the cash flow flowing.

Cabot Farmers' Co-op is enthusiastically and determinedly computerizing, modernizing, and streamlining. In late 1987 construction of the long-planned ninety-three-thousand-square-foot storage facility was completed. Now the production, cutting, aging, and distribution functions, which for years took place at four separate locations, are centralized. Cabot Co-op has entered a joint venture with the large French co-op, Est Lait, to make soft-ripened cheeses in Cabot. The co-op is making fewer commodity cheeses, and more value-added products. To hasten this transition, the co-op has greatly increased its marketing budget. The specialty gourmet market is being courted with the attractively packaged Sharp, Extra Sharp, and Private Stock Cheddars, which have been aged for, respectively, between nine and twelve months; between fourteen and twenty-four months; and more than twenty-four months. A casual collection of names of visitors to the plant has been updated and categorized to form the basis of an effective mail-order program. A slick catalogue featuring Cabot cheeses as well as other Vermont farmstead food products is available at the plant and by mail.

However, the hands-on cheese-making process will remain the same. Despite the inherent problems of being a co-op and of producing a high-quality aged cheese, Alan Parker was adamant. "Vermont Cheddar is white; it is aged; it is of a distinct and robust flavor; and Cabot is committed to making Vermont Cheddar!"

This spicy salad includes the red, white, and green colors of the Mexican flag, so we named it in honor of Mexico's Independence Day. It keeps well and is excellent picnic fare.

3 cups cooked white rice (Basmati or Thai Jasmine for more flavor)
1 small red onion, chopped in ½-inch dice
1 sweet red pepper, chopped in ½-inch dice
1 Anaheim, *poblano,* or other mildly hot green chile, chopped in ½-inch dice*
1 cup cilantro leaves, loosely packed
4 ounces white Cheddar, grated (1 cup)
1 teaspoon cumin seeds, crushed
1 teaspoon salt
Juice of 2 limes
½ cup oil (half olive oil and half peanut oil is preferred)

Combine the rice, onion, pepper, chile, cilantro, and cheese in a large bowl.

In a separate bowl, combine the cumin, salt, lime juice, and oil.

At least 30 minutes before serving, toss together all the ingredients.

*If you cannot find any of these mildly hot peppers, use a sweet green pepper and half of any seeded and minced small hot chile, such as *jalapeño.*

Cinco de Mayo Rice Salad

Serves 6 to 8

Green Beans and Hazelnuts with Cheddar

Serves 4 to 6

This recipe offers a pleasing balance of texture and flavor: the crunchy beans and nuts provide a counterpoint to the melted cheese. The nutty flavor in the Cheddar fuses with the hazelnuts.

1 pound green beans, halved
1 cup hazelnuts (approximately 5 ounces)
¼ cup butter
1 red onion, halved and thinly sliced
¼ cup dry white vermouth
½ teaspoon fresh thyme
Salt and pepper, to taste
6 ounces medium Cheddar, grated (1½ cups)

Parboil the beans in salted water for 1 or 2 minutes, then cool.

Toast the hazelnuts in a 350°F oven for 3 to 5 minutes. Cool and chop coarsely.

In a medium skillet, melt the butter, add the onion, and sauté over low heat until soft. Add the beans and the vermouth. Cook for 3 minutes. Add the thyme, salt, and pepper. Sprinkle with grated cheese, cover the pan, and remove it from the heat. Allow the cheese to melt, approximately 2 to 3 minutes. Sprinkle with toasted nuts and serve.

Northeast Cheddar meets Southwest flavors to warm the souls and stomachs of Americans in any region, in any season.

1 large baking potato, peeled and coarsely chopped
1 large onion, coarsely chopped
2 or 3 fresh red Anaheim or *poblano* chiles, coarsely chopped
1 garlic clove, coarsely chopped
1 teaspoon cumin seeds
3 tablespoons corn oil
1 cup water
2 cups milk
2 cups fresh or frozen corn kernels
¼ teaspoon freshly ground black pepper
1 teaspoon salt
½ pound sharp Cheddar, grated (2 cups)
Fresh cilantro

In a large saucepan, sauté the vegetables with the cumin seeds in oil until the onion is soft. Add the water, cover, and simmer for 15 minutes or until the potato is soft. Add the milk and cook for 3 minutes. Purée in batches in a blender or food processor.

Return to the pot, add the corn kernels and heat gently, approximately 5 minutes. Add the salt, pepper, and cheese. Stir over low heat until the cheese is melted and the soup is hot. Serve immediately, garnished with cilantro leaves.

Cheddar Chile Soup

Serves 6 to 8

Cabot Farmers' Co-op

Cauliflower Caraway Tart

Serves 8

If you prepare the crust, cheese sauce, and other ingredients in advance to assemble at the last minute, plan to heat in the oven longer than the five minutes recommended below. Serve with a green salad and a fresh, light red wine such as a Beaujolais or a rosé.

Crust
1 cup all-purpose flour
½ teaspoon salt
1½ teaspoons caraway seeds, crushed
½ cup sweet butter
2 to 4 tablespoons ice water

Combine the flour, salt, and caraway seeds.

In a processor or by hand, cut the butter into the flour mixture until pea-sized. Add enough ice water to form a ball. Refrigerate for at least 1 hour.

Roll out and line a 10-inch, fluted tart pan that has a removable bottom.

Preheat the oven to 400°F. Line the tart crust with aluminum foil, fill with pie weights, and bake for approximately 10 minutes. Remove the weights and return the crust to the oven to bake for 3 to 5 minutes, until slightly browned. Cool.

Filling
2 tablespoons unsalted butter
1 cup sliced leeks, white part only (about 2 medium)
2 tablespoons all-purpose flour
1½ cups milk
½ pound Cheddar, grated (2 cups)
⅛ teaspoon cayenne pepper
Salt and freshly ground pepper, to taste
1 large head cauliflower, broken into florets and steamed al dente
2 hard-boiled eggs, sliced
1 medium tomato, sliced ¼-inch thick
1 cup whole wheat bread crumbs, browned in 1 tablespoon butter

In a medium saucepan over medium-low heat, melt the butter, add the leeks, and sauté, stirring occasionally, until softened, approximately 8 to 10 minutes. Add the flour and cook, stirring, for 2 to 3 minutes. Pour in the milk slowly,

Cabot Farmers' Co-op

84

stirring all the while. It should thicken in 2 to 4 minutes. When thick, add the cheese, stirring until melted. Remove from heat and add the cayenne, salt, and pepper to taste.

Preheat the oven to 350°F.

Carefully fold the cauliflower florets into the cheese sauce. Fill the tart shell, arrange the slices of egg and tomato on top, and cover with bread crumbs. Warm in the oven for 5 minutes or until heated through. Serve at once.

Orb Weaver Farm

New Haven
Vermont

Orb Weaver Farm

••••••••••••••••••

*New Haven
Vermont*

CHEESE: Orb Weaver
    Vermont Farmhouse
    Cheese
RETAIL SALES: Yes
TOURS: No
MAIL ORDER: Yes

The industrious orb weaver is a spider known for her particular orb-shape web that is visible on the grass in the early morning dew. The two owners of Orb Weaver Farm, Marjorie Susman and Marian Pollack, begin their days in that early morning dew, milking their forty-five Jersey cows. Continuing through the day, they work their four-acre market garden, build and rebuild the structures on their land, make cheese, deliver their products, and then milk their "girls" again that evening.

The gently rolling hills of the dairy land of western Vermont provide a tranquil setting for the rustic, 1790s farmhouse on Orb Weaver Farm. The small herd of Jerseys is carefully tended. As we watched, each contented bovine claimed her own place on the milking stanchion under her own name. Unlike those at most dairies, each cow on Orb Weaver Farm has a name, not a number. Each milking takes at least two hours. As the pampered beauties left the barn, one stopped and stared at us, refusing to move on until Marjorie gave her a little shove, and explained, "She just loves the color of your skirt."

Most of the milk produced each day goes to the making of the Orb Weaver Farmhouse Cheese. The milk is carried from the milking barn to the little cheese house just up the hill. The clean and tidy processing room holds a small vat and other cheese-making equipment purchased from Holland. Here the milk is heated, a starter added and, later, the rennet is stirred in. When the curd forms, the whey is drained out but the curd is not washed. It is salted, cut, and worked by hand with large paddles to keep the curd pieces separate. The salted curd is then transferred to two- and five-pound Gouda molds in which it is pressed to force out the remaining whey.

The next day, the cheeses are removed from the molds and placed in the curing room for approximately one week to dry and form a rind. After this curing period, the cheeses are waxed. Marjorie and Marian choose to age their cheeses for approximately six months before offering them for sale. Their cheese is available in two- or five-pound wheels, or one-pound wedges cut from the five-pound wheels.

Rows of clean shelves filled with neatly arranged rounds and wedges of cheese line the walls of the Orb Weaver curing room. Rounded tops and bottoms form shapes that are simple, soft, and almost voluptuous. An alluring aroma of fresh sweet milk emanating from this charming room completes the picture. Marjorie and Marian formulated and then improved upon their cheese over the years. It is unique in that it is not a washed-curd cheese like Colby, nor is the curd "cheddared" as it is for Cheddar. Their cheese is creamy and mild (not unlike Sonoma Jack), and exceptionally low in salt (they add only one cup of salt to ten pounds of cheese). Marjorie and Marian wanted a cheese that represented their cows and their farm. They have done it. Orb Weaver Farmhouse Cheese is a straightforward, country cheese that certainly reflects the women who make it and the place in which it is made.

The owners of Orb Weaver, now so at home on their farm, were actually born and raised in the cities and suburbs of Northeastern America. Several years ago they met in Massachusetts and found that they shared a common dream to move to the land to farm. Marjorie enrolled in a two-year agricultural course specializing in dairy management while Marian continued her social work as a probation officer and family therapist in Harlem.

In pursuit of their dream, Marjorie found a job milking eighty cows and raising replacement heifers on a dilapidated eighteen-acre farm. In 1982 they bought the farm, which they named after that diligent spider they admired. These women are unique in their community, where it is most unusual to have such a small and diversified farm. Nonetheless, the locals stop to admire their garden and their cows and to buy their cheese, vegetables, and flowers. Besides selling directly from the farm, they deliver their vegetables and cheese to local restaurants. Their cheese can be found for sale in local markets and apple orchards in the area. It can be purchased by mail order and bought in such places as Zabar's and Bloomingdale's in New York City.

These women are living their dream. In doing so, they nurture their ancient, ailing house, their garden, their cows and, of course, their cheese. They have earned the friendship and respect of their farming neighbors, no easy feat for two female city slickers. Is this what they imagine doing for the rest of their lives? Marjorie answered for them both, "We have started playing the lottery but have decided that even if we win, we will still keep our cows and keep making cheese."

Asparagus Salad

························

Serves 4

Asparagus is grown at Orb Weaver Farm. We love this salad of two of the farm's products.

¾ pound asparagus, tough ends removed
4 ounces Orb Weaver Farmstead Cheese
1 cup coarsely chopped walnuts
1 tablespoon balsamic vinegar
1 tablespoon lime juice
3 tablespoons olive oil
1 teaspoon Creole or Dijon mustard
Salt and pepper to taste
Half a red bell pepper, seeded and diced

Preheat the oven to 350°F.

Cut the asparagus into 2-inch pieces and steam until just tender. Cool in ice water.

Cut the cheese to match the asparagus pieces.

Toast the walnuts in the preheated oven until lightly browned, 3 to 5 minutes.

Mix the vinegar, lime juice, oil, mustard, salt, and pepper in a salad bowl. Add the red pepper, asparagus, and cheese. Marinate for approximately 30 minutes.

Mix in the walnuts and serve at room temperature.

Marjorie and Marian eat their cheese every day and avidly seek different ways to serve it. Since they favor Mexican-style flavorings, we dedicate this to them.

1 medium potato, cubed (approximately ½ cup)
4 tablespoons butter
1 small green bell pepper or 1 mild green chile, cubed (½ cup)
1 medium red onion, chopped coarsely (½ cup)
4 eggs, beaten
½ pound Orb Weaver Farmstead Cheese, cut in ½-inch cubes
Chile Sauce (recipe follows)
4 large burrito-sized flour tortillas
4 tablespoons chopped cilantro

Parboil the potato for 5 minutes and drain.

In a medium skillet, melt the butter, add the potatoes, green pepper, and onion and sauté for 4 to 5 minutes until the onion and pepper are softened. Add the eggs and cheese. Scramble until the eggs are just set.

Spread 2 tablespoons of chile sauce in the center of each tortilla. Spoon a quarter of the egg mixture onto the sauce on each tortilla. Roll the tortillas, place on a plate or baking dish, and heat briefly in a microwave or 350°F oven for 5 minutes.

Place on individual plates, spoon half a cup of chile sauce over each burrito, and sprinkle with chopped cilantro.

Chile Sauce

2 ounces large dried California or New Mexican chiles
2 garlic cloves
1 small red onion, sliced
½ teaspoon oregano
¼ teaspoon ground cumin
1¾ cups water

Preheat the oven to 450°F. Place the chiles on a baking sheet and toast them lightly in the preheated oven for 1 to 2 minutes. Do not let them burn. Remove from the oven and cool slightly. Discard the stems and seeds.

In a medium saucepan, bring all the ingredients to a boil. Simmer until soft, about 20 minutes. Cool slightly.

Purée in a blender or food processor and then force the purée through a sieve. Keep warm.

Orb Weaver Burrito

Serves 4

Orb Weaver Farm

Macaroni and Cheese

••••••••••••••••••••

Serves 4

Invariably, when we asked cheese makers for recipes, we received yet another for macaroni and cheese. We took it from there. Here is a colorful version that might almost be recognized as the old American favorite.

1 bunch Swiss chard, white stems discarded
2 tablespoons butter
1 medium onion, chopped
1 can (16 ounces) Italian-style tomatoes, chopped and drained (2 cups)
½ pound spinach pasta, in corkscrew, shell, or macaroni shapes
½ pound Orb Weaver Farmstead Cheese, grated (2 cups)
3 ounces Blue Cheese, crumbled (¾ cup)

Coarsely chop the Swiss chard and steam until just wilted.

Melt the butter in a sauté pan. Add the onion and cook over low heat until soft. Add the tomatoes and remove from heat.

Cook the pasta al dente, 8 to 10 minutes. Rinse with cold water and drain well.

Preheat the oven to 350°F.

Butter a 2-quart baking dish. Place half of the pasta in the dish, layer with half of the tomato mixture, and then with half of the cheeses. Repeat the layers, cover and bake in the preheated oven for 35 minutes.

Orb Weaver Farm

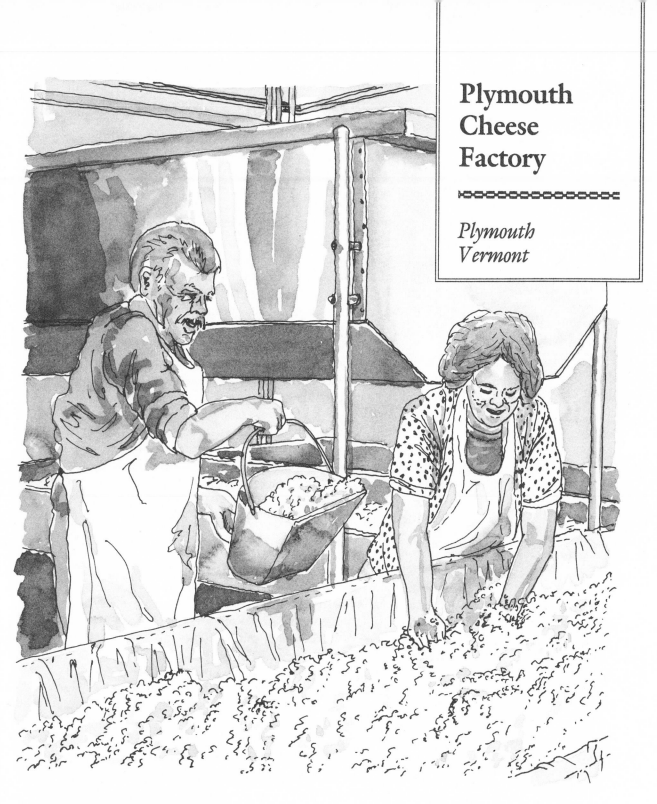

**Plymouth
Cheese
Factory**

*Plymouth
Vermont*

Working the curds vigorously by hand

Plymouth Cheese Factory

━◼━◼━◼━◼━◼━◼━◼━◼━◼━

Plymouth Vermont

CHEESES: Plymouth
  Cheese—Plain, Sage,
  Pimiento, Caraway, and
  Smoked
RETAIL SALES: Yes
TOURS: Yes
MAIL ORDER: Yes

Plymouth, Vermont, has a claim to fame. It was the birthplace of the thirtieth American president, Calvin Coolidge. Here Mr. Coolidge was born, raised, married, sworn in as president and, ultimately, buried. This is a proud little town steeped in history, a history that is thoughtfully preserved. Several buildings dating back to the nineteenth century still stand in Plymouth, maintained in good condition, and open for public perusal.

Summer is the tourist season here, the time of year when the little town comes to life. Visitors come to Plymouth from all over the world, by the busload. We arrived around noon to find a bustling town and lines of people at the Plymouth Cheese Factory. It seemed rather odd after our long drive through the dense and silent country that surrounds it.

The factory was built in 1890 by Calvin Coolidge's father in collaboration with some local farmers to provide an outlet for the increasing supply of milk. From the time of its inception until it was closed in the 1930s, farmers brought their milk in cans each morning.

The president's son, John Coolidge, broke the silence of the shut-down plant in 1960, when he once again opened its doors. After some needed renovation, an addition to the building, and the replacement of old equipment with new, the resurrected cheese factory opened. John's preservation of his grandfather's cheese factory to perpetuate the tradition of the region was celebrated by the townsfolk. The cheese factory not only contributes to the tourist attractions of the town, but also advances the spirit of the community.

Physically, the cheese factory is small, though certainly adequately sized for its production. It is old and quite basic yet remarkably clean and neat. There is a production room, an aging cellar, a shipping and wrapping room, an office, and a salesroom. Visitors watch the cheese-making process from behind a railing.

The cheese produced here is a traditional New England type known as Granular or Stirred-Curd Cheese. Originally, this truly American cheese was produced in the farmhouses of New England. The cheese made at Plymouth is similar to Crowley cheese but with its own characteristic flavor. It is firm yet moist in texture. Granular is a most satisfactory descriptor. The flavor is mild, somewhat similar to that of a young Cheddar.

Besides the original cheese and a smoked variety, Plymouth

offers cheeses flavored with pimiento, sage, or caraway. Sage, a rather unusual choice, flavors a tasty cheese enjoyed by New Englanders with mincemeat pie. We learned that Plymouth has no official recipe for the quantity of sage to be added to the cheese curds. The cheese maker, Arnold Butler, remarked, "We throw it in until it looks right."

Arnold is a large, friendly native of Vermont, who has been making cheese at the Plymouth factory for twenty years now. He knows his craft, from the making of culture through the aging of cheese. He works almost single-handedly, turning out approximately thirty-eight tons of finished cheese each year, and using twelve thousand pounds of milk a week.

Mary Earle, the office manager, has also been with the cheese factory for many years. Her bookkeeping work, like the cheese making itself, is accomplished by hand. All of the twenty thousand mail-order notices are hand-addressed. It would be difficult to imagine a computer in this setting. Besides Mary, two or three local women operate the tasting room, selling cheese to the numerous and seemingly constant visitors. The factory is open six days a week except from the end of November until the beginning of May. No cheese is made in December because all of the employees' energy is focused upon the voluminous holiday mail-order business.

For his Plymouth Granular Curd Cheese Arnold prefers to use milk, purchased from a local creamery, standardized to a fat content of between 3.6 and 3.8 percent. The milk is heated and his culture and rennet added. The curd is formed, cut, stirred, and heated. The whey is removed, then the curds are rinsed. Now the fun begins. It is at this point that Arnold habitually yells, "Help!" Volunteers arrive and, for about half an hour, the curds are worked vigorously by hand. *Worked* means squeezed, pinched, and compressed. This is a high-spirited time for sharing jokes, conviviality, and laughter while getting a serious workout. When Arnold determines that the curds have been massaged enough, he salts them, works them some more, fills the molds, and submits them to the press. Later the pressed cheese is cured and then aged for several months.

John Coolidge showed us the divinely fragrant aging room. Richly aromatic and filled with handsome cheeses, it was unquestionably a treasure house. Mr. Coolidge said, "We are in the same boat as the Vermont farmers, getting ready for winter all year long." The winter for which they are perpetually readying themselves is the month of December when most of those wheels roll out the door, to serve as gifts or for holiday entertaining.

Clearly, the Plymouth Cheese Factory survives today by reason of John Coolidge's dedication to an historic perspective. He is not interested in building a fortune, but rather, in carrying on a tradition. The profits, we imagine, are marginal and the work hard. His employees enjoy some cheerful lamenting about the hard work but possess a genuine pride in what they do. These are good, honest people who make a good, honest product. Plymouth is unpretentious, practically homespun. Such a substantial, authentic cheese amply reflects the enduring, steadfast, rugged character of Vermont.

Plymouth Cheese Factory

We discovered how delicious the combination of Smoked Plymouth Cheese, cool, sweet grapes, and lightly poached chicken can be. This salad is particularly suitable for summer dining.

1½ pounds chicken breasts (4 whole)
1 tablespoon peppercorns (Szechwan preferred)
½ cup sliced blanched almonds
1 cup seedless red grapes
4 green onions, diced
4 ounces smoked Plymouth Cheese, grated (1 cup)
1 garlic clove, minced
Juice of 1 lemon
2 tablespoons sherry
5 tablespoons olive oil
1 bunch watercress, washed, dried, and thick stems removed

Place the chicken breasts and peppercorns in a saucepan with enough cold water to cover. Bring to a boil over high heat, boil for 1 to 2 minutes, turn off the heat, and allow to steep for 10 minutes. Remove the chicken from the water and cool.

When cool, bone and skin the breasts and cut the meat into 1-inch cubes.

Toast the almonds in a 350°F oven for approximately 5 minutes or until toasty brown.

Place the chicken, grapes, three-quarters of the almonds and a quarter of the chopped onion in a medium bowl.

In a food processor or blender, mix the cheese, garlic, lemon juice, sherry, and oil until smooth. Toss the watercress and remaining onions with a quarter of the cheese dressing. Arrange on a serving platter, leaving a circular space in the center. Mix the remaining dressing with the chicken mixture. Mound the chicken in the middle of the greens, sprinkle with the remaining almonds, and serve at room temperature.

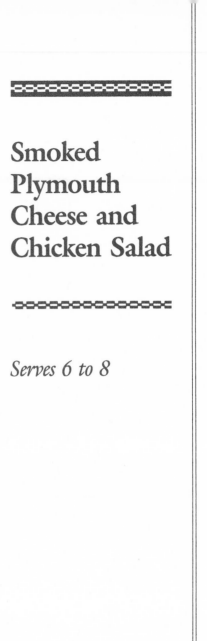

Smoked Plymouth Cheese and Chicken Salad

Serves 6 to 8

Plymouth Cheese Factory

Wild Mushrooms in Cheese Pastry

Serves 4

These mushroom-filled pastries are a meal in themselves. Serve with a green salad and crusty bread.

Pastry
4 ounces Plymouth Cheese, grated (1 cup)
4 tablespoons unsalted butter, cut into pieces
1½ cups all-purpose flour
⅛ teaspoon minced fresh rosemary
½ teaspoon minced fresh thyme
3 to 5 tablespoons ice water

Mix all the ingredients together in a food processor or by hand just until a ball forms. Cover the dough and chill for at least 30 minutes.

Filling
1 to 2 ounces dried *shiitake* mushrooms
3 tablespoons olive oil
¼ cup shallots, chopped
1 teaspoon fresh thyme, chopped
⅛ teaspoon fresh rosemary, chopped
½ cup red wine
1 tablespoon brandy
2 tablespoons butter
½ pound fresh mushrooms, cleaned and sliced
½ pound Plymouth Cheese, grated (2 cups)
2 tablespoons milk or 1 egg, beaten

Cover the dried mushrooms with very hot water. Soak until soft, approximately 20 minutes. Drain and reserve the liquid.

In a medium skillet, heat the oil over medium heat. Add the shallots and herbs and sauté until soft. Add the wine, half a cup of mushroom liquid, and the brandy. Cook over high heat to reduce the liquid to approximately 2 tablespoons.

Remove and discard the stems from *shiitake* mushrooms. Slice and add them to the shallot mixture.

In another skillet, melt the butter and sauté the fresh mushrooms until soft. Combine the 2 mushroom mixtures. Cool.

Preheat the oven to 400°F. Cut the dough into 4 equal sections. Roll into 4 very thin circles.

Add the cheese to the mushroom mixture. Arrange one quarter of the mixture slightly below the center of each

Plymouth Cheese Factory

98

pastry circle. Fold the top half of the pastry over the filling and seal the edges, cutting away any excess.

Place on a cookie sheet, seam-side down. Brush lightly with milk or beaten egg and bake in the preheated oven for 18 to 20 minutes or until the crust browns lightly. Serve hot.

Serve these at cocktail hour and watch them disappear. Be sure to not overcook the little morsels.

    ½ pound smoked Plymouth Cheese, grated (2 cups)
    4 ounces butter
    1 cup all-purpose flour
    ¼ teaspoon salt

Combine all the ingredients in a food processor. Mix thoroughly until a ball forms. If working by hand, blend until smooth with wooden spoon.

Divide the dough into 32 balls, each approximately 1 inch in diameter. Place on cookie sheets, cover, and refrigerate for at least 2 hours or overnight.

Just before serving, preheat the oven to 450°F. Bake for 8 to 10 minutes, allowing the domes to brown lightly. If they are overcooked, these rich little mouthfuls will taste bitter.

Smoked Cheese Domes

Makes about 32 domes

Plymouth Cheese Factory

Fennel, Olive, and Cheese Salad

Serves 4 to 6

An autumn lunch sparkles with this fresh, crunchy, and colorful salad. Add a cup of soup and a slice of dark rye bread.

3 tablespoons red wine vinegar
6 tablespoons fruity olive oil
¼ teaspoon salt
½ teaspoon freshly ground pepper
2 small bulbs fennel, trimmed and thinly sliced
1 small red bell pepper, diced
½ cup Greek olives, pitted and chopped
1 small red onion, chopped
½ cup coarsely chopped cilantro
4 ounces Plymouth Cheese, cut into matchsticks

In a medium serving bowl, mix the vinegar, oil, salt, and pepper. Add the fennel, red pepper, olives, onion, cilantro, and cheese. Toss lightly and serve.

Hawthorne Valley Farm

Ghent
New York

Placing the cheeses on shelves in special curing rooms to age

Hawthorne Valley Farm

~~~~~~~~~~~~~~~~~~~~~~

Ghent
New York

CHEESES: Raclette, Caraway, Emmenthaler, Gruyère, Quark
RETAIL SALES: Yes
TOURS: Yes; call ahead
MAIL ORDER: Yes

A great and serious experiment in the integration of head, heart, and will is taking place in a wide fertile valley in Columbia County, New York. Situated amid pastures, crop land, wooded hills, and clear streams is the Hawthorne Valley Rudolf Steiner Farm School. The purpose of the farm is to awaken and cultivate the full capacities of the well-rounded human being through education, the arts, and agriculture. The Rudolf Steiner theory of biodynamics, an advanced organic method of enhancing soil fertility and animal health, is the force that unifies the farm and the individuals who work it.

In the mid 1970s a group of teachers in conference with some farmers in the area purchased the 350-acre farm. They were fueled by their visionary goal of providing an integrated living system. Their ideal was to allow school children from New York City the experience of life on a true farm. The inner-city children stay for week-long visits, while local children attend the school. The children are introduced to a highly mechanized form of farming. The land is worked to provide feed for the various animals, including a herd of fifty Holstein and Brown Swiss dairy cattle, and grain for the bakery at the farm store.

The dairy herd provides milk for the cheese and yogurt produced at the farm. The cows are milked in the barn, not far from the cheese production rooms, and their fresh milk is piped into a bulk tank where it awaits its next journey into a beautiful, large, old copper kettle. Here the milk is heated and culture and rennet are added. To make the Gruyère and Emmenthaler, the curd is allowed to set, then cut and heated to 115 degrees. Then the whey is pumped to the barn to feed the cows and pigs. The remaining curd is scooped into a huge cheesecloth that is manipulated into a bag. The bag is hoisted with block and tackle and wheeled to the drainage table. Here the curd is pressed in a frame to remove the free whey before the curd mass is cut into blocks and placed in cheese forms. The forms are turned three times that day, then allowed to rest overnight.

The next day the nine- and fifteen-pound wheels of cheese are turned out of the molds and immersed in a salt brine for twenty-four hours. For two weeks the Gruyère is scrubbed vigorously every day to encourage the growth of surface mold. After this period, it is aged for six months before it is sold. To encourage propionic gases, the Emmenthaler is rubbed daily for a few days with a wet salt. It is aged in a seventy-degree "warm room" for one month, then moved to a cooler (fifty- to fifty-five-degree) room for another month.

The Hawthorne Valley Farm cheese maker, Tom Myers, has a long history with the farm. In the spring of 1980, after a cheese-making apprenticeship in Switzerland, Tom came to Harlemville to work on the farm and to make cheese. After the better part of a year, he moved nearby and for five years produced Camembert with milk he purchased from the farm. He returned to Hawthorne Valley Farm after a second European apprenticeship and has served as the cheese maker since April 1986. Tom has always been interested in cheese making as his *métier,* devoting himself to it as to a craft rather than as a business. Tom believes, "All the technical knowledge in the world will not make you a good cheese maker. It takes years of experience. In this country, without a tradition to fall back on, it takes even longer."

We tasted three impressive Hawthorne Valley cheeses: Raclette, Emmenthaler, and Gruyère. They are all high-quality, brawny farm cheeses, very similar to their European namesakes. The semisoft Raclette, encased in a rough, khaki-colored rind, is pale golden yellow in color. Its creamy, yielding texture is balanced by its full, buttery flavor. It is milder than most imported Raclettes, with a fresh, spring-milk flavor. The Emmenthaler is the brightest golden yellow of the three. It has a hard, yellow and waxy rind surrounding the body of a cheese characterized by large irregular shiny holes and a typical nutty and mild Swiss cheese flavor. Tom's Gruyère is the strongest flavored and also the longest aged of the three. Six months of aging gives the cheese a complex taste— a sharp tingle and a walnut flavor. The cheese is ivory in color, has tiny irregular eyes, and is enclosed in a tawny rind like sandpaper.

Approximately half of the cheese produced at the farm is sold at the Union Square Farmer's Market in New York City. The rest is sold at the farm store and through mail order. Tom speaks of rounding out the product line with Camembert and Taghkanic (a washed-rind cheese still being developed) and of diverting half the farm's milk supply into yogurt production.

The success of the Hawthorne Valley cheeses is, in part, a reflection of the biodynamic system that helps support their existence. Tom perceives the stumbling block for American specialty cheese to be that the price the consumer is willing to pay can never justify the cost of production. At least here there is a community and the biodynamic structure that includes the bakery, the school, the people, and the farm, all contributing to the success of the whole. There is no doubt in our minds, however, that these delicious and distinctive cheeses more than amply carry their share of the load.

Here is an unusual combination of the flavors of the Northeast. Serve as a tasty accompaniment to a mid-winter roast beef or pork. Accompany with a Merlot or Cabernet.

2 leeks, white part only, washed thoroughly
½ pound jicama, peeled*
1 large carrot
½ pound turnip, peeled
½ pound rutabaga, peeled
2 tablespoons butter
2 tablespoons apple cider vinegar
¼ cup pure maple syrup
½ pound Gruyère, grated (2 cups)
Salt and pepper to taste

Preheat the oven to 350°F.

Cut the vegetables into ¾-inch dice. Steam together until tender, 15 to 20 minutes. Drain and set aside.

Over low heat, melt the butter in a small shallow pan. Add the vinegar and maple syrup. Simmer until the mixture thickens, 3 to 4 minutes.

Arrange half of the vegetable mixture in a shallow baking pan. Cover with half of the cheese. Pour over half of the syrup mixture. Salt and pepper lightly. Cover with the remaining vegetables, then the remaining cheese, and drizzle with the remaining syrup. Sprinkle lightly with salt and pepper. Cover, then bake in the preheated oven for 25 to 30 minutes until bubbly. Serve hot or warm.

*Jicama grows like a tuber, underground. It is irregularly shaped, has a thick brown skin and a crunchy, somewhat sweet interior, similar to a water chestnut. It can be purchased in many supermarkets.

Winter Root Vegetable Stew

Serves 4 to 6

Hawthorne Valley Farm

Bulgur Salad

Serves 4 to 6

The crunchy crispness of this salad is best appreciated if the dish is served soon after it is made. It is, however, delightful as picnic fare. Serve with beer or a chilled rosé wine.

½ cup virgin olive oil
2 tablespoons sherry vinegar
Salt to taste
Generous grind of black pepper
2 cups cooked and cooled bulgur
½ cup finely sliced carrots
½ cup finely sliced celery
½ cup minced green onion
½ cup minced parsley
½ cup thinly sliced radishes
½ cup watercress, thick stems removed, chopped
4 ounces Gruyère or Emmenthaler, diced
1 small head leaf lettuce, washed and dried

Combine the oil, vinegar, salt, and pepper in a mixing bowl. Add the bulgar, carrots, celery, green onion, parsley, radishes, watercress, and cheese. Toss thoroughly. Serve at room temperature on a bed of lettuce.

A pinwheel slice of this hearty bread tastes as good as it looks. Serve a generous portion with a bowl of steaming vegetable soup for a satisfying meal. The bread is excellent also as a quick, nutritious breakfast.

1 cup warm water
1 teaspoon sugar
1 package active dry yeast
2½ cups all-purpose flour
½ cup whole wheat flour
2 tablespoons oil
½ teaspoon salt
4 ounces any Hawthorne Valley cheese, grated (1 cup), at room temperature
4 ounces Cream Cheese, at room temperature
2 tablespoons minced chives
½ teaspoon caraway seeds
Cornmeal
1 egg, beaten

Mix ¼ cup water, the sugar, and the yeast in a small bowl. Let rest for 10 minutes.

In a food processor or by hand, mix the yeast mixture, flours, oil, salt and the remaining ¾ cup water. Knead for 10 minutes or until elastic. Place in an oiled bowl, cover, and let rise in a draft-free area until doubled in bulk, 1 to 2 hours.

Mix the cheeses with the chives and caraway seeds. On a floured surface roll out the dough to a rectangle measuring approximately 10-by-18 inches. Spread the filling evenly over the surface of the dough, leaving a half-inch edge all around. Roll up the rectangle, starting with a short side. Pinch the ends and the seam to seal. Place the bread roll, seam-side down, on a baking sheet sprinkled with cornmeal.

Let the bread rise for 45 to 60 minutes.

Preheat the oven to 350°F. Cut a slit ⅛ inch wide down the middle, along the top of the loaf. Brush with beaten egg. Bake for 55 to 60 minutes in the preheated oven. Cool before slicing.

Hawthorne Farm Rolled Cheese Bread

Makes 1 loaf

Hawthorne Valley Farm

New World Raclette

Serves 4

The legendary Swiss dish, Raclette, based on the cheese after which it is named, includes boiled potatoes, sausages, pickled gherkins, and onions. Traditionally the cheese is softened by the heat of a fireplace. As it warms and softens, it is sliced and served with the other components of the dish. In our New World Raclette, we use the barbecue, American ingredients, and Hawthorne cheese.

2 yams, washed and cut in ½-inch rounds
2 or 3 small white or red potatoes, washed and cut in ½-inch rounds
1 sweet potato, washed and cut in ½-inch rounds
4 mildly hot chiles, such as *poblano* or Anaheim
2 red onions, sliced ½-inch thick
4 duck sausages (available in delicatessens and specialty food stores)
1 pound Raclette in a wedge
Small jar of Mexican pickled cactus (available in many supermarkets)

Light a barbecue grill.

Steam the yams, potatoes, and sweet potato until just tender. Grill the chiles over medium-hot coals until the skins are blistered. Cool, peel, and remove the seeds. Grill the onions, yams, potatoes, sweet potatoes, and sausages. Place the cheese, set on aluminum foil or in a small pie tin, on the grill. Meanwhile arrange all the grilled vegetables, sausages, and pickled cactus on a serving platter. When the cheese is softened and warm, but not melted, slice in generous portions and serve. Let the diners help themselves to vegetables and sausage. Keep the remaining cheese warm, near the grill, for subsequent servings.

Rawson Brook Farm

························

Monterey Massachusetts

CHEESES: Monterey
   Chèvre in five
   varieties—Plain, Chive
   and Garlic, Thyme and
   Olive Oil, Unsalted,
   Peppered Log
RETAIL SALES: Yes
TOURS: By appointment
MAIL ORDER: Yes

Since the early 1980s, dozens of small-scale or farmstead goat-cheese producers have materialized in the United States. This vocation has provided an opportunity for many to support themselves, albeit often minimally, while living in a place and in a style close to their hearts. Though presently, there seem to be little pockets of goat-cheese making activity—in California, Washington State, the Midwest, and in the Northeast—eventually every farming community might be favored with at least one producer.

Rarely have Americans chosen to raise goats as a means to financial success. Instead, people buy one or two goats as an addition to a small family farm and eventually their herds multiply. Goat raisers tend to be quirky, hard-working "do-it-yourselfers," devoted to their animals. Some of them become goat-cheese makers.

At present there are more than fifty such farmers who are making goat cheese on a small scale, and Americans' blossoming interest in goat cheese encourages their efforts. Most run farmstead operations, in which all of the milk and the cheese is produced on the farm. Here we tell of two who typify the genre, both of whom farm in the Northeast: Barbara Reed of Little Rainbow Chèvre, and Susan Sellew and Wayne Dunlap of Rawson Brook Farm.

Susan and Wayne bought their first goat for seventy-five dollars many years ago, packed her in their car, and wondered where their remaining twenty-five dollars would take them. Since then they have never been without goats; their herd now numbers over fifty. They live with their goats in Monterey, Massachusetts, where they have cleared five acres of forested land, terraced a garden, and built a goat shelter and an attractive little cheese-making facility. They share an enduring love for their goats, whose health and happiness is of prime importance to them. They refuse to use chemicals in their goats' feed or on their land. Indeed, their life and work is fully integrated: they live on the land they work, in the house they built, from revenue generated by cheese they make out of milk from their own goats.

Barbara Reed and her husband, Thomas, bought their first goats rather than a horse for their daughter. Now they have more than 120 goats as well as three horses, and various other farm animals. The Reed family lives a rural life on their organic farm, and abide by an indomitable do-it-yourself credo.

Barbara's decision to make cheese was a result of her son's allergy to cow's milk and his liking for cheese. With no local sources of information on making goat cheese, Barbara learned her craft through experimentation and reading. Friends and neighbors who tasted the results encouraged her to start selling her cheeses.

Both Rawson Brook Farm and Little Rainbow Chèvre have small cheese houses directly connected to their dairies, the source of the milk. The cheese making is performed with care and attention. Milk is pasteurized, culture and coagulant added, and curd allowed to form. Then the curds are either gathered into bags to hang and drain or ladled into molds, where they drain. Beyond that, Barbara ages some cheeses and inoculates them with blue mold; the cheeses from Rawson Brook are sold fresh.

Both businesses sell to individuals by mail order as well as to stores and restaurants. Susan and Wayne encourage visits to their farm and enjoy selling their products directly to consumers. Susan explains that their young, fresh cheeses "are easy for people to eat and accept. Some don't even know it's goat cheese." We found their cheeses delightfully light and fresh, leaving a remarkably clean impression on the palate. They know their customers and like to introduce goat cheese to newcomers, especially to children. They have received remarkable local support for their endeavor and count their neighbors as regular clients. To celebrate the completion of their cheese-making building, they invited the community to an open house. They still talk about their surprise when 350 people arrived instead of the expected fifty. The open house has become an annual event, popular with summer tourists as well as with the locals.

Barbara sells directly to the consumer at the Greenmarket in New York City once a week. She leaves for the market at 4:30 A.M. and returns late in the evening. Barbara's day may be arduous, but it allows her to sell her cheeses personally to large numbers of people. She relishes the opportunity to display the full range of her production, including her popular, robust, full-flavored Blue Goat Cheese.

These cheese makers are proud of their work and especially of their independence and self-sufficiency. Sacrifices made to achieve the success they now enjoy are both expected and accepted as part of a commitment to a life style that to some of us may seem difficult and tedious. People who willingly work

Little Rainbow Chèvre

••••••••••••••••••••

*Hillsdale
New York*

CHEESES: Chèvre Logs, various aged cheeses, and Blue Goat Cheese
RETAIL SALES: Yes
MAIL ORDER: Yes
TOURS: By appointment

*Two Northeast Farmstead
Goat Cheese Producers*

III

long and hard to live the way they want and to reach their goals are continuing proof that the pioneering aspect of the American spirit has not faded.

The following recipe is a contribution from Robin Lenz, chef at 1896 House, Williamstown, Massachusetts. The cheese may be eaten, with French bread, as soon as it has been prepared, or marinated to be enjoyed later. It will keep for two or three days.

4 ounces fresh Goat Cheese
Half a small red onion, thinly sliced
Half a bay leaf
½ teaspoon thyme
½ teaspoon rosemary
1 garlic clove, diced
Freshly ground black pepper, 3 or 4 turns of a peppermill
4 tablespoons cognac
½ cup dry white wine
½ cup fruity olive oil

Form the cheese into a log and, with a sharp knife, slice it into 8 rounds and place them on a plate.

Combine the sliced onion, bay leaf, thyme, rosemary, garlic, black pepper, cognac, and wine in a saucepan and bring to the boil. Reduce the mixture to a syrup. Add the olive oil and swirl to mix. Pour the mixture over the slices of Goat Cheese. Serve at room temperature.

Marinated Goat Cheese with Cognac, Red Onion, and Herbs

Serves 4

Two Northeast Farmstead Goat Cheese Producers

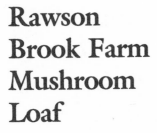

Rawson Brook Farm Mushroom Loaf

Serves 4 to 6

This loaf, devised by Susan Sellew, is a favorite at the Rawson Brook Farm. It may be served as an appetizer, a snack, or accompanied by a crisp salad.

8 or 10 cultivated button mushrooms, finely chopped
2 tablespoons olive oil
8 ounces fresh Goat Cheese
¼ cup all-purpose flour
¼ cup bread crumbs
1 egg
¼ teaspoon thyme

In a medium skillet, sauté the mushrooms in olive oil until soft. Cool.

Preheat the oven to 400°F.

Combine the mushrooms with the cheese, flour, bread crumbs, egg, and thyme and form into 2 loaves, each 2 inches in diameter. More flour or bread crumbs may be necessary.

Place on a baking sheet and bake in the preheated oven for 30 minutes, or until golden brown. Serve warm or at room temperature.

John Elkhay of the New England Truffle Company contributed the recipe for this deliciously decadent confection. Ask your guests to guess the secret ingredient.

    6 ounces semisweet chocolate
    4 ounces unsalted, soft Goat Cheese
    ¼ cup honey
    1 teaspoon vanilla extract
    1 tablespoon finely chopped lemon zest
    ½ cup Dutch-process cocoa

Melt the chocolate over low heat in a double boiler or in a microwave oven. Add the honey and Goat Cheese. Stir until smooth. Add the vanilla and lemon zest. Chill the mixture for several hours.

    Form 24 small balls. Roll in cocoa.

On those summer evenings when you are grilling anyway, why not make this delectable dish to start things off? It is quick, easy, and unusual.

    1 large eggplant
    Olive oil
    Salt and pepper
    6 ounces herbed Goat Cheese, at room temperature

Light a charcoal grill.

    Cut the eggplant lengthwise into ½-inch slices. Brush each slice lightly with olive oil. Lightly salt and pepper each side. Brown both sides of the eggplant slices on a hot grill. Remove from the grill and spread sparingly with cheese. Roll up the slices and secure them with toothpicks.

    Place the rolls on the grill briefly to warm through, taking care not to burn them. Serve hot.

Chocolate Truffles with Massachusetts Goat Cheese

Makes 24 truffles

Grilled Eggplant with Herbed Goat Cheese

Serves 4

Two Northeast Farmstead Goat Cheese Producers

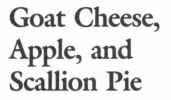

Goat Cheese, Apple, and Scallion Pie

Serves 6 to 8

Here is our adaptation of an unusual recipe that comes from Ralph Perrotti, Lawrence Kolar, and Edith Broduer of Café in the Barn, Seekonk, Massachusetts. We like this savory concoction for brunch or lunch.

½ cup butter
1 cup all-purpose flour
½ cup sour cream
3 large tart apples (Granny Smith or pippin), peeled and coarsely diced
½ cup chopped scallions (green onions)
10 ounces unsalted, soft, fresh Goat Cheese
1 cup heavy cream
3 eggs
⅛ teaspoon nutmeg

To prepare the crust, cut the butter into the flour by hand or in a food processor. Add the sour cream. Mix until it forms a ball. Refrigerate for 30 minutes.

Preheat the oven to 450°F. Roll out the dough into a 10-inch circle and use it to line a 9-inch pie pan. Fill with the apples, scallions, and Goat Cheese. Combine the heavy cream, eggs, and nutmeg and pour this mixture over the other ingredients.

Bake in the preheated oven for 15 minutes. Decrease the temperature to 350°F and bake for 30 minutes more, until the mixture is set. Serve warm.

Two Northeast Farmstead Goat Cheese Producers

Filling molds with curds

Valley View Cheese Co-op

◆━◇━◆━◇━◆━◇━◆━◇━◆━◇━◆

South Wayne Wisconsin

CHEESES: Brick—
Caraway, Low-Salt;
Muenster–Raw-milk,
Low Salt, Caraway
Caraway
RETAIL SALES: No
TOURS: No
MAIL ORDER: Yes

"If every person in this country would eat one more pound of cheese per year, we could sell 260 million pounds more cheese," asserted our host. We had arrived fifteen minutes earlier and were chatting with his wife, Susie, while expecting the arrival of the man whose reputation had preceded him. Wild Billi Lehner of Forgotten Valley is famous for his opinions about everything from the world situation to the ideal way to make cheese. Susie was adding the final touches to a caldron of aromatic mushroom soup destined for the lunch we were about to share. Though we were gathered in a little house above a cheese plant in southern Wisconsin, the atmosphere was more than vaguely reminiscent of some rural French farms visited years ago. Billi burst in and greeted us warmly.

Before lunch he had to attend to a few details in the factory, so we accompanied him. His sons were performing various tasks in the small, organized rooms. They seemed to be serious and committed hard workers who knew how to move, yet they possessed a sense of humor and camaraderie. When we remarked upon this, Billi laughed, "Work harder for less! Work for Billi!" A short while later, when we were seated around the table, Billi shared some of his concerns. "You can't make good cheese if the cows are not healthy," opened a diatribe about the deplorable state of America's cows. In the quest for efficiency and productivity, our cows are pushed to mature earlier and to produce more milk. They have been bred to be larger and taller than their ancestors, the cause of now-common serious birthing problems. Twenty years ago, a cow attained the ripe age of three years before calving; today they are expected to produce milk at the age of two. A two-year-old cow does not yet possess a fully developed body, likening her predicament to that of a fourteen-year-old girl giving birth to a child. Today's farmers feel that, if they are to survive financially, they must force their cows into early service. Considering the rising cost of feed, veterinarian bills, labor, and the purchase price of the animal, it generally takes one and a half lactations before the farmer breaks even on his investment. Billi asserts that, by the time a cow is five years old, she is broken down because she has been pushed all her life for maximum production.

More important for this cheese maker, he feels that her milk is inferior, lacking in flavor and color. It cannot compare to the milk produced by a contented bovine grazing on the lush pastures in the mountains of Switzerland, her diet augmented from time to time with a little hay. "Cows must go on pasture. That's the way God intended it."

"We are all in the same sack," Billi exclaimed. "We feel forced to produce, produce, produce—nay, overproduce! And to do it faster, faster, faster. Then we have to fight to stay in business. In order for a small cheese factory to survive, it is necessary to specialize and to make a better, higher quality cheese than the competitor makes. And it is impossible to make good cheese if cows are not healthy."

Wisconsin has undergone some significant changes in the last thirty or forty years. A large number of the small family-owned cheese plants that could not survive in this atmosphere were sold to larger companies. Billi muses over whether this indicates that only large companies can ultimately survive in America. He believes it is unfortunate for the future of specialty cheese in America that, for the most part, these large companies tend to produce a rather bland, undistinguished, albeit often good-quality, product.

Billi has been a cheese maker for about thirty years. He always thought that he should have been a farmer, given his love of animals, especially of cows. But in Switzerland after the war, farms were expensive. Cheese making seemed a more reliable way to earn a living. He served a three-year cheese-making apprenticeship in Lucerne, which he described to us. "The first year you don't even touch the milk. You don't even look at it. You scrub. Every week you spend an afternoon at a dairy school. Each year you apprentice at a different place." At the ripe age of nineteen, Billi had completed his apprenticeship and was a cheese maker.

Struck by wanderlust, Billi went to France and then traveled all over Europe. After a few years he landed in Wisconsin, America's famous cheese region. There he managed a large cheese factory for twenty-one years, until it was time for a change. The Valley View Co-op in South Wayne, Wisconsin, hired Billi as the cheese maker and manager of their old and tiny factory. Built in 1850, the picturesque, European-styled, Valley View Farm in Forgotten Valley is one of the oldest in Lafayette County.

Each day, with help from his sons, Billi processes between forty and sixty thousand pounds of milk, turning it into Brick, Muenster, Farmer's, and Caraway Cheese. Susie analyzes the milk in their laboratory, testing it for phosphatase, pH, and antibiotics. As is traditional in Switzerland, the family works together.

In response to our queries about his philosophy of cheese making, Billi said, thoughtfully, "You have to love what you do to work like this. You have to put in something extra. That something extra is time. Cheese has to be made with feeling. There are very few perfect cheese makers around because people don't have time any more. When you cut the curd, you can feel the life in that curd: how hard, how soft, and how the bacteria is working. You have to know when is the right time to cut the curd. And you have to be willing to wait fifteen minutes or half an hour if necessary because this makes a big difference in the flavor."

Every year Billi wins prizes for his outstanding cheeses. For example, in 1981, his cheese was chosen Best of Class in the Brick division in the Biennial United States Cheese Championship Competition. In 1982, he won the Governor's Sweepstakes in Wisconsin. In 1983, he won again at the United States championship, with the highest score of all the cheeses entered in this prestigious event. And, in 1984, his cheese was awarded the Best in Class in the Muenster division in the Biennial World Champion Cheese Competition. Billi thinks that is "pretty good" for a little factory. He still remembers the day he made the cheese that won the United States championship in 1983. "It was a Sunday. Everything just clicked right that day. I made it slowly. In time. I let it go a half hour longer, so it wouldn't dry up. It was just right."

American cheese lovers can expect many delights in the future from Billi Lehner. He has been experimenting with the production of Havarti cheese. He has begun producing more low-sodium and low-fat cheeses. He has opened a second cheese factory, owned in partnership with a Chicago-based distributor of Mexican food products. No doubt there are numerous other projects buzzing about in his active mind.

Valley View cheese is packaged under various labels. The richly flavored, smooth-textured raw-milk Muenster is distributed through natural food stores under the name Billi's Monster Cheese. The other cheeses, which to our taste are less distinctive than the Raw-milk Muenster, can be found under their "Forgotten Valley Cheese" label, but much of their cheese is packaged under labels other than their own. Presently, these Valley View cheeses are sold in Pennsylvania,

New York, Michigan, Wisconsin, and Illinois.

Billi is keenly aware of the serious problems faced by our farmers and the need for Americans to value and support our important resource, farming. He speaks of the increasing mediocrity of our mass-produced foods. However, he also recognizes our tremendous potential to improve our lives and the lives of others throughout the world. Billi ponders these issues continually, discussing them with all who will listen. He is distressed at our present situation, but remains essentially an optimistic man. "We need some new answers. But there is hope. We are still a young country and we are changing."

Forgotten Valley Popovers

Makes 1 dozen popovers

Susie Lehner, an enthusiastic cook, finds novel uses for Billi's cheese. Here is our version of one of her favorite ideas.

1 cup all-purpose flour
1 teaspoon salt
2 eggs, beaten
1 cup milk
2 to 3 tablespoons melted butter
4 ounces Muenster or Brick, cut into 12 chunks

Add the flour and salt to the eggs and mix lightly. Add the milk and melted butter. Mix quickly but thoroughly; the less the mixture is beaten, the better.

Pour the batter to fill buttered muffin tins a quarter full. Add one chunk of cheese, then add batter to fill two-thirds full.

Place in a cold oven. Turn the oven to 425°F and bake for 30 to 35 minutes. Serve hot.

Gratin of Leeks

Serves 4

4 leeks, white part only, washed and cut into ¼-inch rounds
2 tablespoons butter, cut into small pieces
2 tablespoons dry vermouth
Freshly ground pepper, to taste
½ teaspoon salt
½ teaspoon fresh, or ¼ teaspoon dry, tarragon
3 ounces Muenster, coarsely grated (¾ cup)

Preheat the oven to 350°F.

In a small, uncovered casserole, combine the leeks, butter, vermouth, salt, pepper, and tarragon. Bake in the preheated oven for 30 minutes. Remove from the oven and sprinkle with cheese. Place under broiler for 2 or 3 minutes, until the cheese is bubbly.

Valley View Cheese Co-op

For another novel recipe we thank Michael Clark. Calamari (squid), an increasingly popular and available seafood, in this preparation is an attractive anchor for a meal. Accompany it with steamed greens and a lean Chardonnay or Sauvignon Blanc wine.

2 cups bread crumbs
½ pound Muenster, grated (2 cups)
16 small calamari, cleaned, and tenderized*
1 cup all-purpose flour, seasoned with salt and pepper
2 eggs, beaten
1 cup peanut oil
2 lemons, quartered

Combine the bread crumbs and cheese. Dredge the calamari in the seasoned flour, shaking off the excess. Dip into the beaten eggs, then coat thoroughly with bread and cheese mixture, pressing the coating into the calamari with the palm of your hand. This may be done in advance and the calamari refrigerated until needed.

Pour half of the oil into a large skillet. Place over high heat until the oil starts to smoke. Carefully place the coated calamari into the hot oil without letting the pieces touch. Fry for no longer than 30 seconds. Flip and fry the other side for no longer than 30 seconds. (When squid is overcooked, it becomes rubbery.) Add more oil, if necessary, to fry all pieces. The fillets should be golden brown. Serve immediately, with lemon wedges.

*To tenderize calamari, place the pieces between two sheets of plastic wrap. Pound them with a mallet until softened and thinned, but not shredded.

Calamari Muenster

Serves 8

Baked
Summer
Squash

Serves 6 to 8

2¼ pounds summer squash, diced
3 tablespoons butter
2 garlic cloves, minced
1 small fresh red chile, minced
1 teaspoon salt
½ teaspoon freshly ground pepper
2 tablespoons chopped fresh basil
½ pound Muenster, grated (2 cups)
1 cup walnuts, chopped
1½ ounces Parmesan, grated (⅓ cup)

Preheat the oven to 350°F.

Steam the squash until softened slightly, for approximately 3 minutes. Drain thoroughly, squeezing out as much moisture as possible.

In a medium skillet, melt 1 tablespoon of the butter. Add the garlic and chile and sauté for 2 to 3 minutes. Add the squash. Mix in the salt, pepper, and basil. Add the Muenster and mix thoroughly. Turn into a buttered baking dish.

Mix the remaining 2 tablespoons butter with the walnuts and Parmesan. Crumble onto the squash mixture. Bake in the preheated oven for 10 to 15 minutes.

Maytag
Dairy Farms

Newton
Iowa

Maytag
Dairy Farms

~~~~~~~~~~~~~~~~~~~~

Newton
Iowa

CHEESES: Blue, Cheddar,
   Edam
RETAIL SALES: Yes
TOURS: Video tour
MAIL ORDER: Yes

Past the mammoth Maytag appliance factory east of Des Moines, Iowa, down a picturesque country road we found a small, modern office building. Here we met Jim Stevens, vice-president and manager of the Maytag cheese operation. Jim took us further down the lane to a quaint, well-maintained old farm for a tour of the cheese-making facilities. We were curious to learn how the washing machine Maytags had become the Blue Cheese Maytags, and Jim was more than happy to inform us.

In the early 1920s, Elmer H. Maytag, son of the founder of Maytag Company, started his lifelong hobby of raising Holstein-Friesian cows. Elmer died in 1940, leaving his dairy herd as well as three model dairy farms to his sons, Frederick II and Robert. Fred and Bob liked cows well enough, but not enough to keep them as a hobby. The sons decided to make those cows pay their own way, or else. Their search for a use for the milk took them to Iowa State University, where a method for producing Blue Cheese from homogenized cow's milk had just been developed. As luck and timing would have it, behind the Maytag dairy lay a hillside in which caves could be dug to provide the cool, humid aging rooms required for the maturation of the blue mold. The University provided the expertise, Maytag provided the facilities and staff, and the first cheeses were produced in 1941.

Jim Stevens, who has been with Maytag since the early years, remarked, "It is easier to make a product than it is to develop your customers." From the outset, the marketing plan was to sell directly to consumers. Luck and timing were evident once again, for already in place was a nationwide marketing network for the sales of Maytag appliances. When dealers and sales representatives appeared at the home office, they were, as a matter of course, given a tour of the cheese facility. Once back in their communities, they boosted the cheese as well as the appliances. Word spread to food editors in major cities and a demand was created. Although Maytag has remained small, it is perhaps the most well known and well respected of all Blue Cheese producers. The Maytag fame has resulted almost entirely from word-of-mouth promotion, and an extraordinary 80 percent of the cheese is sold through mail order.

Maytag Blue Cheese is made almost entirely by hand and fully aged in the caves behind the dairy. First, the cream is separated from the milk and subjected to two thousand pounds of pressure to break up and disperse its molecules. It is then added back to the skim milk. This milk is pumped into vats, heated to ninety degrees, and allowed to reach the proper acidity before rennet is added. The curd forms and is cut and drained of whey. The *Penicillium Roqueforti* mold is sprinkled over the curds, which are then scooped into four-pound stainless steel hoops. These curd-filled hoops are placed on draining tables and hand-turned repeatedly until the cheese is formed. Once formed, the cheese is salted, then punctured to create air pockets, which are essential for the development of the blue mold. Blue cheese requires more salt than most other cheeses, as salt encourages growth of the mold.

Next, the wheels are placed in the curing cave. Four weeks later they are scraped, coated with wax, and moved to the aging cave where they rest, protected, for six months, twice as long as most commercially produced Blue Cheese. Blue Cheese ripens best in a cool, moist atmosphere and these caves, dug into an Iowa hillside, provide nature's helping hand.

Today, the third generation of Maytags owns the cheese business. The children of Fred Maytag bought out the other family members. They hold executive positions and are called upon when major decisions are necessary. Fritz Maytag is chairman of the board and spokesman for the family. He also owns the Anchor Steam Brewery in San Francisco, which produces a high-quality, European-style specialty beer. We have tasted Maytag Blue accompanied by Anchor Steam beer and found the combination superb.

The people at Maytag had long harbored a dream to produce other cheeses. Recently they went back to the University at Ames, Iowa, for help. The result is a wonderful white Cheddar and a flavorful Edam. Interest in these cheeses is growing but the Maytag Blue produced in this picture-book setting is by far the stellar cheese. Several years ago the late James Beard, the noted American food authority and writer, became enamored of Maytag Blue. He staged a contest in one of his cooking classes pitting the Maytag cheese against some of Europe's best Blue Cheeses. As Jim Stevens said, "Well, you can guess which cheese won, or I wouldn't even be telling you."

Blue Stew

Serves 6

One September afternoon in a Paris restaurant, we feasted upon a simple, traditional mélange similar to the following. Whenever we prepare our Blue Stew here at home, we fondly recall that soul-warming meal.

1 pound carrots
1 pound onions
1 pound potatoes
¼ cup butter
2 large garlic cloves, coarsely sliced
5 cups chicken or vegetable stock or water
½ teaspoon coarsely ground black pepper
1 whole cabbage, approximately 2 pounds
1 teaspoon salt
9 ounces Blue Cheese

Clean, peel and cut the carrots, onions, and potatoes into large, 2-inch chunks. Melt the butter in a 3- to 4-quart saucepan or Dutch oven. Add the vegetables and garlic, cover, and cook over medium heat for 10 minutes. Add the stock or water and black pepper. Simmer for 20 minutes. Core the cabbage and cut it into eighths. Add the cabbage and salt to the vegetables. Simmer for 10 minutes.

Just before serving, crumble 1½ ounces Blue Cheese into each of 6 bowls. Ladle the stew into the bowls and serve piping hot.

Our favorite caterer, Michael Clark, concocted this salad, so bright in color and flavor.

16 medium, fresh beets
½ pound Blue Cheese
½ cup sour cream
4 tablespoons red wine vinegar
2 tablespoons chopped fresh dill

Boil the beets until just tender. Cool and peel. Slice thinly, then cut into julienne strips. Crumble the cheese over the beets. Add the sour cream, vinegar, and dill. Toss gently. Taste and adjust the seasonings. Chill. Serve on a bed of green lettuce or spinach.

The classic Blue Cheese accompaniments, port and walnuts, are combined here in a versatile spread that is ideal for hors d'oeuvres. For a change, enjoy this rich-tasting spread on crisp, cool pears, celery, carrots, or other crudités.

2 ounces Blue Cheese
1 ounce butter
2 tablespoons port
Freshly ground pepper, to taste
3 to 4 ounces walnuts, chopped
3 slices whole wheat bread
1 teaspoon finely chopped chives

Thoroughly mix the cheese, butter, port, and pepper. Add the walnuts. Toast the bread and cut the slices into quarters. Spread with the cheese and nut mixture and sprinkle with chives.

Blue Beets

Serves 4

Blue Cheese Toasts

Makes 12 canapés

Maytag Dairy Farms

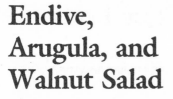

Endive, Arugula, and Walnut Salad

Serves 4

1 tablespoon sherry vinegar
1 tablespoon minced chives
Freshly ground black pepper, to taste
6 tablespoons crème fraîche*
2 ounces Blue Cheese, crumbled
1 cup walnuts, chopped
4 Belgian endives, sliced crosswise ¼-inch thick
2 cups arugula, coarsely chopped

Combine the vinegar, chives, pepper, and crème fraîche in a small bowl. Gently mix in the cheese. Toss the dressing with the walnuts, endive, and arugula. Serve immediately.

*If crème fraîche is not available, substitute 4 tablespoons heavy cream mixed with 2 tablespoons buttermilk.

Chicken Liver Salad

Serves 4

An uncommon approach to the traditional combination of liver, bacon, and onions, this warm salad is suitable for an entrée at lunch or first course at dinner.

6 tablespoons olive oil
1 tablespoon champagne vinegar
¼ cup minced, cooked bacon
2 ounces Blue Cheese
Freshly ground black pepper, to taste
¾ pound chicken livers, quartered
1 large shallot, minced
1 bunch leaf lettuce

Combine 4 tablespoons of the olive oil with the vinegar, bacon, Blue Cheese, and pepper.

In a medium sauté pan, heat the remaining 2 tablespoons olive oil over medium-high heat. Add the chicken livers and shallot and cook for 4 to 5 minutes, or until the exterior of the livers is crisp but interior still medium rare.

On a serving platter, arrange the lettuce leaves and place the livers on top. Pour over the cheese and bacon dressing and serve warm.

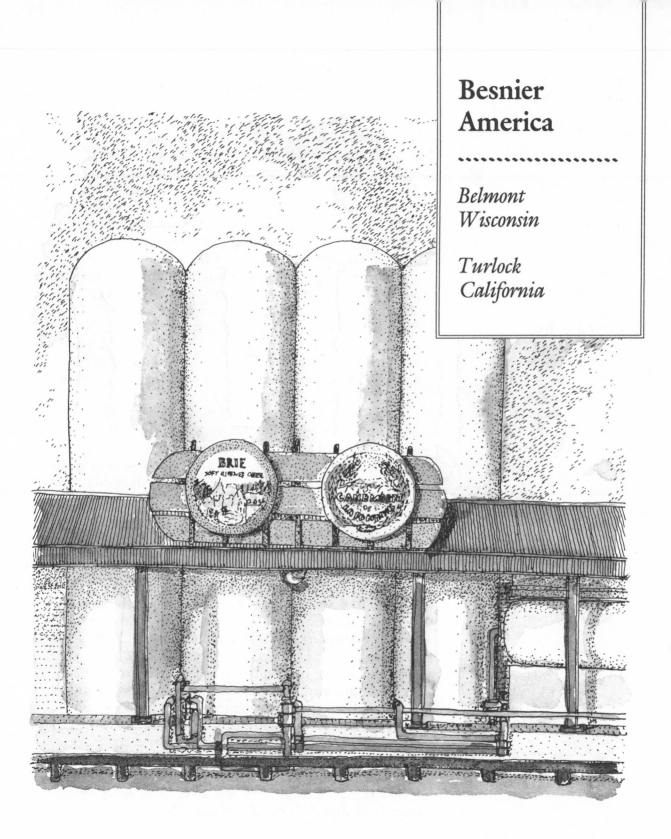

Besnier America

....

*Belmont
Wisconsin*

*Turlock
California*

Besnier America

························

*Belmont
Wisconsin*

*Turlock
California*

CHEESES: Brie,
    Camembert, Très Blue,
    Belmont d'Or
RETAIL SALES: Yes
TOURS: No
MAIL ORDER: No

Americans' increasing consumption of cheese has not escaped the attention of European cheese producers. Nor have they disregarded the fact that Americans have displayed a particular interest in specialty cheeses. The Europeans have noticed this trend because it is they who have supplied most of the stuff. By tradition, Europeans have been appreciative consumers of large quantities of cheese. They have been pleased to spread the word to us and even more pleased to make a profit in doing so. In short, the Europeans have discovered an enthusiastic market for their wondrous and various cheeses, and have only just begun to take advantage of it.

A few far-thinking and adventurous European cheese companies have not been content merely to supply an eager and hungry American market from their factories across the Atlantic. They have ventured forth with a new plan. Why not set up shop and produce European-style cheese in America itself? In the late seventies and early eighties, the first of these innovators took the plunge. Others will come to our shores, as it is an obvious and logical move.

Besnier was one of the first. Currently one of the largest and fastest-growing cheese companies in France, Besnier would naturally choose to capture the American market. The company was established in 1933 by André Besnier, a maker of Camembert in Normandy. To begin with, he made only enough cheese to supply his tiny village. As appreciation of his products grew, so did his market, and then his supply. Today the Besnier company boasts thirty-six factories, including one that is the largest facility of its kind. Besnier employs between five and six thousand people and supplies as much as 40 percent of the Camembert consumed in France.

In 1980, Besnier purchased a cheese plant in Belmont, Wisconsin. Famous as America's dairyland, Wisconsin has its own cheese-making tradition. Once there were almost a thousand small cheese factories throughout the state. They bought much of the local milk and their end product, usually Cheddar, was consumed locally. As our transportation systems advanced and our cheese-making technology improved, the little local cheese factories began to disappear. Now there are only about three hundred left and the attrition continues. How ironic, yet encouraging, that European cheese makers are coming to revive a part of our dairy industry!

By 1982, the Besnier plant was in business. All of the equipment, as well as the cheese maker himself, had been transported from France. The entire operation was to be overseen by Claude Bellanger. Mr. Bellanger is certainly qualified, if not, in fact, overqualified for this position, as he has been in the cheese business for more than twenty years. As a teenager he worked at a dairy in Normandy. If his father had had his way, his son would have become a surgeon, but Claude was not enthralled with that prospect. When the manager of the dairy convinced the young man that he should choose a career in the dairy industry, he decided to pursue his education at the University at Nancy, famous for its courses in cheese and dairy technology. In time he became manager of Besnier's largest plant. He recalls the vision of thirty-five million Camembert cheeses in the curing room on any given day!

Mr. Bellanger was much taken with the challenge of managing Besnier's pilot plant in Wisconsin. The Wisconsin facility is a fraction of the size of many of the company's French factories, the equipment and methods not of the latest technological complexity, and the size of production quite modest. However, the invitation to work with American milk, American labor, and an exclusively American market interested him. The process has not been entirely without wrinkles, but Mr. Bellanger is pleased with the progress they have made. He reports that the plant is running smoothly now and everything is under control.

His original obstacles in America stemmed from lack of control over his milk source, difficulties in marketing, and some uneasiness, perhaps some suspicion, in the local community. Mr. Bellanger is duly impressed by the quality of milk in Wisconsin, and particularly by its cleanliness. He objected to the way in which it was handled: it was pumped from the farm's bulk tank into the truck that came to collect it; pumped from the truck to the reception center; pumped into another truck; and, from there, pumped into the silos at his plant. He feels that all this pumping is detrimental to the final product because it breaks up the butterfat in the milk. He quickly arranged to buy milk directly from local farmers and to make sure that any co-op milk he received was not subjected to the extra pumping at the reception center.

Besnier's marketing office in New York handles both its French and American products. The company has advertised the American cheese extensively, using, among other media, full-page advertisements in national magazines. The emphasis has been on the "natural" aspect of the product and the fact that it is made in Wisconsin. The advertisements imply that, because the cheese is a French product made in America, one can have the best of both worlds. Besnier's advertising is apparently effective: sales have grown considerably, along with the marketing efforts.

Bellanger was greeted at first with some dismay by the local citizens. They were anxious about the looming specter of competition in an already ailing cheese market. In time their fears were allayed as they realized Besnier's products did not compete directly with local cheeses. In fact, Besnier improved the state of the local economy by providing jobs. Bellanger is pleased with his American employees, finding that they have a "better spirit" than do their counterparts across the Atlantic.

The factory in Belmont is presently producing an array of sizes and flavorings to broaden the line of Brie and Camembert. Both cheeses are available in four-ounce, eight-ounce, one-pound, one-kilo and two-kilo sizes; either natural or flavored with herbs, onion, pepper, or bacon. The company offers cheeses with both a 50 percent and 60 percent butterfat content and have found that the latter is overwhelmingly preferred in America. Control, the most desired component in cheese making, is maintained in an in-house laboratory that tests both the milk and the cheese. The starter, made right there at the factory, is added to the pasteurized milk. Once the milk has attained the desired pH level, it is poured into vats. Coagulant is added and soon afterward the curd is cut and pumped out of the vat into molds. The molds are turned twice by hand, then moved to a cooler room. There they are dipped into a salt brine, and receive their dose of *Penicillium,* the mold responsible for the particular texture and flavor of Brie and Camembert.

The cheeses age in special rooms where the temperature— and humidity—are controlled. The white mold appears gradually. When the mold growth has reached the desired stage, the cheeses are wrapped in special paper and boxed in little wooden boxes, both imported from France. Perhaps someday the boxes will be made here, but for now there is not enough demand for little wooden cheese boxes to merit a commitment to such an enterprise.

Besnier cheeses sold in America (whether made abroad or domestically) are tailored specifically to the Besnier perception of American taste; it is whiter, has a more prolific mold growth, and a longer shelf life than the cheese produced for the French. In France the cheese tends to be creamier and is, perhaps, allowed to mature longer. This difference in style probably owes its origin to the dictates of American distributors seeking to guarantee a longer shelf life, rather than to a response to American taste, whatever that may be.

In May 1987, Besnier America opened a second manufacturing plant in Turlock, California, that enabled the firm to triple its production. This fifty-thousand-square-foot facility is the largest Brie and Camembert factory in the West. In the summer of 1988, the company added two new products to its line: Très Blue, a triple crème blue-veined variety that is 70 percent butterfat and is soft, rich, and unctuous, and Belmont d'Or, a semisoft cheese with eyes like those in Swiss cheese. Nobody will say what is next, but it would come as no surprise to us if Besnier cheese (and perhaps butter) plants someday dot the landscape of America. That would certainly signal a change in America's cheese consumption and would contribute to an atmosphere in which other specialty cheese producers could thrive.

Brie Pancake

Serves 4

Rich-tasting yet light, our Brie pancake is a versatile dish. We have especially enjoyed it, in both its sweet and savory versions, as an unusual Sunday breakfast.

3 eggs
¾ cup milk
¾ cup all-purpose flour
3 ounces Brie, thinly sliced, rind removed
Salt to taste*
¼ cup butter
½ cup minced chives
Cayenne pepper

Preheat the oven to 425°F.

Mix the eggs, milk, flour, Brie, and salt in a food·processor or blender for approximately 10 seconds. Put the butter in a 10-inch ovenproof omelet pan and place it in the hot oven. Remove it from the oven when the pan is very hot and the butter is bubbling and just beginning to brown.

Quickly pour the egg mixture into the pan and return it to the oven immediately. Bake for approximately 20 to 25 minutes. The sides of the pancake will rise above the pan and the pancake will be solid, crisp, and lightly browned. Serve immediately, garnished with minced chives and sprinkled with cayenne.

To make a sweet version, omit the chives and cayenne. Instead, serve the pancake sprinkled with powdered sugar and garnished with fresh fruit, jam, or a fruit purée.

*This is *really* optional: we found the Brie provides enough savor; some of our recipe testers did not.

Quickly prepared and just as quickly devoured, this version of the ever-popular baked Brie is visually appealing with its bright tri-color presentation. Encourage your guests to dip in and enjoy it.

8 ounces Brie
3 or 4 large basil leaves, finely chopped
3 dried oil-packed tomatoes, finely chopped
5 fresh tomatoes, peeled, seeded, and finely chopped
4 tablespoons olive oil
2 shallots, finely chopped
1 tablespoon fresh thyme leaves
3 tablespoons champagne vinegar
¾ pound fresh spinach, stemmed, washed, and dried
French bread

Slice the Brie in half horizontally. Spread the basil and dried tomatoes on the bottom half. Replace the top and set the cheese aside. Simmer the fresh tomatoes over medium heat until the liquid is reduced. Keep warm. Preheat the oven to 350°F. Have ready an attractive serving platter.

Prepare a warm dressing for the spinach: heat the oil, shallots, and thyme over low heat. When the shallots are soft, gently mix in the vinegar. When the mixture is hot, pour it over the spinach leaves and toss thoroughly. The hot dressing will wilt the spinach.

Place the Brie in the oven on a piece of foil or in a small pan. Heat for 3 to 4 minutes. Spread the reduced fresh tomatoes in the center of the serving platter and arrange the wilted spinach in a circle around the tomato. When the Brie is warm, remove it from the oven and place it on the pool of warm tomato. Serve immediately with slices of toasted or fresh French bread.

Wilted Spinach and Brie

Serves 4 to 6

Besnier America

Camembert Tarts

Serves 4

These pretty little tarts make a delectable first course. Small enough to both pique and satisfy that start-of-the-meal appetite, they are also interesting in texture and color.

1 sheet frozen puff pastry
½ pound Camembert
½ cup pistachio nuts, coarsely chopped
3 medium red peppers, roasted, peeled, seeded, and diced
2 large garlic cloves, diced
½ teaspoon freshly ground pepper
3 tablespoons fresh cilantro, parsley, or basil, chopped

Preheat the oven to 400°F.

Roll puff pastry out to a thickness of ¼ inch. Cut into quarters and line four 6-ounce ramekins. Secure the dough over the lip of the ramekins. Prick the bottom and sides of the dough with a fork. Cut the remaining dough into decorative shapes for the ramekin tops. Bake the pastry-lined ramekins and the pastry tops in the preheated oven, for 10 to 15 minutes or until they are puffed and brown.

Remove and discard the Camembert rind. Cut the cheese into ½-inch dice. Lightly toast the nuts, 3 to 5 minutes. Mix the cheese, nuts, red peppers, garlic, pepper, and cilantro thoroughly and fill the ramekin shells. Bake for 8 to 10 minutes. Remove from the oven, decorate with the tops, and serve immediately.

Camembert and Calvados both originate in the same province in France—Normandy—and naturally complement each other. The marriage of flavors is best if the Camembert is allowed to marinate in the Calvados for the full twenty-four hours.

2 tablespoons plus 1 teaspoon Calvados (French apple brandy)
8 ounces Camembert (1 whole cheese)
½ cup walnuts, finely ground
2 pippin apples, sliced into eighths

Pat 2 tablespoons of the Calvados onto the Camembert. Set the cheese aside for at least 30 minutes or up to 24 hours.

Preheat the oven to 400°F. Pat the ground walnuts onto the cheese. Sprinkle with the remaining 1 teaspoon Calvados. Place in the freezer for 30 minutes.

Bake in the preheated oven for 10 minutes, until the nuts are lightly browned. Serve immediately, with sliced apples.

Calvados-Spiked Camembert

Serves 4 to 6

Besnier America

Dipping curd from a copper kettle—2,500 pounds of milk on the way to becoming a 200-pound wheel of cheese

Mueller's Cheese House— Sugarcreek Dairy

=========

Sugarcreek
Ohio

CHEESE: Swiss—Mild,
  Medium, and Sharp
RETAIL SALES: Yes
TOURS: Yes
MAIL ORDER: Yes

In the Amish country, the agricultural areas of Pennsylvania and Ohio farmed by the Amish people, the paved roads are characterized by an uneven, indented trail in the center of each lane, the product of something other than ordinary modern vehicles. The black, horse-drawn buggies driven by dark-clad, bearded men and bonneted women are hauntingly reminiscent of our frontier-settler ancestors. The film, *Witness,* made in 1985 by Peter Weir, provided many Americans with their first exposure to the Amish and their unusual life style. However, this bucolic area has always received visitors appreciative of the simple, fresh, and bountiful family-style meals served by farm wives. Friends who traveled here in their childhood wax lyrical about such exotica as dried corn, scrapple, shoofly pie, *schmier-käse,* and apple butter slathered on fresh homemade bread—the food we all wish our mothers used to make.

The Amish eschew modern conveniences. They use no electricity, do not drive cars or engine-driven farm equipment, and do not wear zippered clothing. Yet, they are prosperous farmers. Initially, the Amish settled in Pennsylvania and Ohio, but now there are communities in almost every state of the Union. As farming families throughout the country can no longer eke out a living, the Amish, undeterred, buy the ailing farms, and work them successfully in their own fashion.

Amish dairy farmers near Sugarcreek, Ohio, supply milk to the area's small cheese companies. They milk their cows by hand, pour the milk into ten-gallon milk cans, and cool the cans in water baths. They have no use for refrigerated milk tanker trucks or way-station tanks, there is no pumping from one giant tank to another. Transportation for the cans is provided by the cheese factories. The cheese makers are faced with special considerations in using Amish milk, such as the operation and maintenance of outmoded can-washing machines and the challenge of working with unrefrigerated milk.

Most of the local cheese plants are owned by second- or third-generation descendants of German immigrants. We visited Paul Mueller of Sugarcreek Dairy, Ed Steiner of Ed F. Steiner, Inc., and Elvira and Gary Indorf of Kidron Swiss Cheese Factory. They all make Swiss Cheese in, more or less, the old-fashioned way.

Paul Mueller's factory can be found in the heart of tourist-oriented Sugarcreek, a village dominated by a German-Swiss motif. "Roll Out the Barrel" blares from loudspeakers on every corner. Until recently, Sugarcreek Dairy was one of the few remaining facilities to use the polished and shining old-fashioned copper kettles to make cheese. Ed Steiner's plant, in the nearby town of Baltic, is a simple, sparkling tile and brick building erected in 1911. In 1978, Steiner switched from copper to the more modern stainless steel vats. The Kidron plant, larger and slightly more technologically advanced, is equipped with the same open stainless steel, eighteen-hundred-gallon vat system as is Steiner's.

All three cheese makers use the same basic system for making their Swiss Cheese. Milk is standardized for fat content, poured into copper kettles or stainless steel vats and heated to ninety-three degrees. Starters and rennet are added. Twenty-five to thirty minutes later, when it "smells and feels right," the curd is cut with hand-held slicers. Then the curd is cooked to a temperature of 122 to 144 degrees. After approximately one hour, the curd is gathered with scoops made from large pieces of cheesecloth or porous plastic and poured into square or round molds. Though traditionally the shape of Swiss cheese is round, wholesalers and retailers today demand 200-pound blocks, claiming there is less waste when cut. All three of our Ohio cheese makers have had to accede to the demands of progress. Once formed, the large blocks or rounds of cheese are salt-brined for one to two days. The blocks are wrapped in plastic for aging; the rounds, unwrapped, are turned and wiped each week. It takes about three weeks for the holes to begin to develop and about five to six weeks for them to form completely.

Ed Steiner gave us a quick lesson in the art of determining the quality of Swiss Cheese. The secret is in the holes: they should be well formed, shiny, elastic, and evenly dispersed. The use of raw milk and seasonal changes in the cows' diet can cause differences from one batch of cheese to another. Much variation in color and flavor is tolerated, but the holes must always be right. All three cheese makers lamented the lack of acceptance of these variations and the constant demand for more consistency.

This dairy area of Ohio was formerly dotted with hundreds of small cheese plants, but relatively few remain. Steiner's plant may well be the oldest continuous family operation in the area. Ed's grandfather came directly from Switzerland to Baltic, Ohio, bought a farm, and began making cheese there.

Ed F. Steiner, Inc.

Baltic
Ohio

CHEESE: Swiss
RETAIL SALES: No
TOURS: No
MAIL ORDER: Christmas only

Kidron Swiss Cheese Factory, Inc.

Kidron
Ohio

CHEESE: Swiss
RETAIL SALES: Yes
TOURS: No
MAIL ORDER: No

Ed F. Steiner, Inc.

He moved the cheese-making operation to a separate plant in 1895 and to the present site in 1903. Ed shared fond memories of his mother's stirring curds in a copper kettle over a wood fire, and visions of her dress with an ever-present singed hem.

Paul Mueller's father was a cheese maker but Paul, not planning to follow the family tradition, became a baker when he returned from the armed forces. Later he took a position with the Ohio Swiss Cheese Association. In his dry, deadpan manner, he explained how he foolishly expressed a slight interest in the Sugarcreek Dairy Co-op and, before he knew it, was its cheese maker. Now he produces and sells cheese for the members, who are farmers supplying milk to the co-op.

In 1949, Erwin Fieni arrived from Switzerland. He bought the present Kidron plant in the early 1950s and is still involved, now primarily with quality control. Elvira, one of his three daughters, and her husband, Gary Indorf, are in command. In her youth, Elvira was a tomboy who liked hanging around the plant, never dreaming she would someday run the place. More and more, that is exactly what she is doing. She is responsible for bookkeeping, sales, check disbursement, and general business management. Gary is the cheese maker. Typical of the profession, he works six days a week ceaselessly from 3:00 A.M., when the first milk is delivered, until around 4:00 P.M., when he takes his leave. When we visited them, they were planning a rare luxury, an outing with their three children, so Gary was going to cut out early—maybe 1:00 P.M.

The Indorfs, Steiner, and Mueller know and respect one another. Important to them all is their Ohio Swiss Cheese Association and their participation in the yearly fall Swiss Cheese Festival. Paul Mueller confided that his one wish is someday to win the Grand Prize for the best cheese at the Festival.

The relationship between the cheese makers and their Amish neighbors, while not particularly social, appears to be honest and respectful. It is symbiotic: the Amish, lacking electric refrigeration, cannot produce Grade A milk and must sell their milk for a lower price. That slightly lower price allows these small factories to survive.

You may search as long and hard as you wish, but you will probably not find Swiss Cheese under the label of Mueller, Steiner, Fieni, or Indorf. These cheeses are sold primarily to

A Trio of Ohio Swiss Cheese Producers

144

wholesalers who, in turn, sell it to supermarket chains. None-theless, all of these cheese makers actively promote their cheeses. Paul Mueller has the factory store in Sugarcreek where tourists may visit and view his "old-time" method of cheese making. The Indorf plant in Kidron is more of a nuts and bolts factory. Ed Steiner has a novel approach. His wife, Dorothy, a talented organist, accompanies him on tours of supermarkets where their cheese is sold. Kind, personable Ed passes out samples and explains his time-tested process while Dorothy plays a portable organ.

The future for these small operations is uncertain. Paul Mueller has purchased two eighteen-hundred-gallon vats to replace his copper kettles. This alteration of procedure has changed his life: he used to work twice as hard to produce half as much as he does now. He is relieved that the work is a little easier, so that as he ages, he will be able to continue to do it. Ed Steiner is thinking about retirement but has no children to inherit his business. Perhaps he will sell to two Amish men who have worked for him for years. Elvira and Gary Indorf are young and energetic, not yet haunted by the concerns of age. They all face the same problems. Some will survive, others will not. But it is clear that for most, there is one truism. As Ed Steiner frankly admitted, "If it weren't for the Amish, I wouldn't be able to make cheese."

Dried Sweet-Corn Pudding

Serves 6

Dried corn is an Amish specialty, found throughout Pennsylvania and Ohio. It is packed by the John F. Cope Co., Inc., Rheems, Pennsylvania 17570. Contact them to find out where it is sold. This pudding makes a tasty side dish.

½ cup dried corn
2 tablespoons melted butter
¾ cup milk
¼ teaspoon salt
¼ teaspoon freshly ground pepper
½ cup chopped onions
2 teaspoons fresh thyme
1 egg
3 ounces Swiss Cheese, grated (¾ cup)

Preheat the oven to 350°F.

In a food processor, chop the dried corn into large pieces; this will take approximately 15 seconds. Add 1 tablespoon of the butter, the milk, salt, pepper, onions, thyme, and egg. Process for approximately 5 seconds, until just mixed. Gently mix in the cheese.

With the remaining 1 tablespoon of butter, coat the insides of six ½-cup ramekins. Divide the mixture among the ramekins and bake in the preheated oven for 30 minutes.

Swiss Cheese, mild and nutty, lends itself well to marination. Here the walnut oil underscores the nuttiness of the cheese and the mustard and vinegar contribute some piquancy. The addition of toasted walnuts to this salad further emphasizes the nutty flavor.

½ cup walnut oil
2 tablespoons balsamic vinegar
1 tablespoon Dijon mustard
Salt and pepper, to taste
4 ounces Swiss Cheese, cut into 1-inch squares, ¼-inch thick
1½ cups dandelion greens, washed and cut into thirds
1½ cups red-leaf lettuce, washed and torn
1 red pepper, roasted, peeled, seeded, and sliced into 1-inch lengths
½ cup walnuts, toasted for 5 minutes in a 350°F oven

In a small bowl, mix the walnut oil, vinegar, mustard, salt, and pepper. Marinate the cheese in this dressing for 1 hour at room temperature. Toss the dressing and cheese with the greens, red pepper, and walnuts.

Ed Steiner recollected his father's practice of serving chunks of Swiss Cheese, onions, and beer to employees for lunch. The combination appealed to us and we expanded upon it.

1 small sweet onion, sliced into 4 rounds
2 tablespoons butter
2 slices rye bread
4 ounces Swiss Cheese, sliced thickly
German or Dijon mustard, to taste
Freshly ground pepper, to taste

In a small pan, over medium heat, sauté the onion in butter until just soft. Lightly toast the rye bread. Generously spread mustard on the bread. Place two sautéed onion rounds on each slice of bread. Top with cheese.
   Heat under the broiler until the cheese melts. Top with freshly ground pepper and accompany with a cold beer.

Country Salad

Serves 4

The Steiner Sandwich

Serves 2

A Trio of Ohio Swiss Cheese Producers

147

Sugarcreek Spaghetti

Serves 4 to 6

Paul Mueller's favorite use of Swiss Cheese is with spaghetti. We had never considered this possibility. We played with the idea and ended up with this subtly sweet and spicy invention.

1 large torpedo onion, cut in half lengthwise and thinly sliced lengthwise
8 tablespoons butter
¼ teaspoon fresh thyme
1½ tablespoons minced fresh chives
1 cup white wine, preferably Riesling
1 pound spaghetti
½ pound Swiss Cheese, grated (2 cups)
Freshly ground black pepper, to taste

In a medium pan, sauté the onions in butter over low heat until soft, about 20 to 30 minutes. Add the herbs and wine. Cook for 30 seconds and remove from heat.

Cook the spaghetti until al dente. Drain and place in a serving dish. Add the cheese to the onion and wine mixture, stirring until just melted. Toss with the spaghetti, season with black pepper, and serve.

This hearty, stick-to-the-ribs, one-dish meal reflects the heritage of the German and Swiss Midwesterners we met. Cold winter nights become warmer with this casserole, which might be accompanied by green salad and a hearty red wine or beer.

    1 celery root (approximately 1 pound), peeled
    1½ pounds potatoes
    1 small onion
    1 pound smoked sausage
    ½ pound Swiss Cheese, grated (2 cups)
    1½ cups half-and-half or milk
    Salt and pepper to taste

Preheat the oven to 425°F.

In a food processor or by hand, slice the celery root, potatoes, onion, and sausage the same size. In a 2- to 3-quart casserole dish, layer half of each ingredient, then half of the cheese. Lightly salt and pepper. Repeat, finishing with a layer of cheese. Pour the half-and-half over the casserole.

Cover and bake in the preheated oven for 30 minutes. Lower the oven temperature to 400°F, uncover the casserole dish, and bake for another 30 minutes. Remove from the oven, and let the casserole rest for 10 minutes before serving.

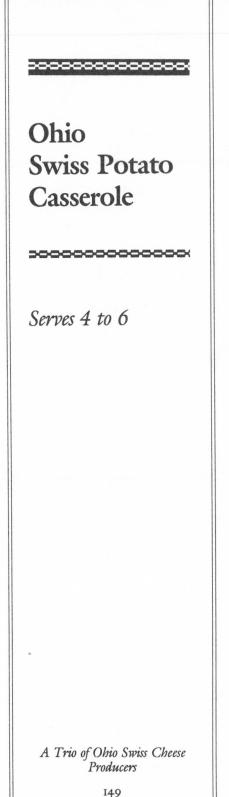

Ohio Swiss Potato Casserole

Serves 4 to 6

A Trio of Ohio Swiss Cheese Producers

Aligot

Serves 6

Aligot is a hearty and filling traditional dish from the Auvergne region of France. Our version uses American-made cheeses in place of the French Cantal. You might enjoy it served with spicy, coarse sausages as it is served there. Be warned, however, that to obtain a fine, silky thread of cheese and potato requires vigor!

2 pounds russet potatoes, peeled and halved
4 tablespoons butter
3 or 4 large garlic cloves, peeled
Freshly ground black pepper
Salt (optional)
½ pound Swiss Cheese, grated (2 cups)

Boil the potatoes for 15 to 20 minutes, or until soft. Add the butter and whip until very smooth. Transfer to a heavy copper or enameled iron saucepan. Using a garlic press, squeeze the garlic cloves into the potato. Add the black pepper and optional salt. Then add cheese and mix thoroughly, always stirring in the same direction, over low heat. As the cheese combines with the potatoes, the mixture becomes stretchy. Continue mixing and stretching, pulling as if you were making taffy, until the mixture is hot and smooth. Serve directly from the pan onto individual plates.

**Kolb-Lena
Cheese
Company**

*Lena
Illinois*

Kolb-Lena Cheese Company

wwwwwwwwwwwwww

Lena
Illinois

CHEESES: Brie,
   Camembert, Feta, and
   Baby Swiss
RETAIL SALES: Yes
TOURS: No
MAIL ORDER: Yes

What would you do if you were the only child of a cheese-making family, had worked in the cheese plant all your life, and when you were eighteen, discovered that you would rather be an artist? That dilemma faced Dorothy Demeter, the grandaughter of Fred Kolb, who had founded the family business. Hard-working cheese makers are a pragmatic lot. Dorothy's father insisted that his only daughter go to college and learn something that pays and not fool with that silly artist stuff. That pragmatism, as well as cheese, must have been running through Dorothy's veins. After a few art classes in college, she, too, decided that she should apply herself to something she knew she could do and do well. She entered the Iowa State University's dairy and cheese-making program and found herself in a man's world: in the early fifties, it was not easy for women to make careers in fields that had traditionally been open only to men.

At the time, there were only twenty women in the entire agricultural school, and Dorothy was the only woman in the dairy department. Now, Dorothy was no shrinking violet. Having grown up during World War II, she had gained experience in the cheese factory. She worked in the plant both before and after school and vividly recalls the day she walked into her classroom with her cheese-plant apron still covering her school clothes. Despite the difficulties she encountered at Iowa State, Dorothy completed the course and in the process met her husband.

Jim Demeter left his home in Greece to go to school in America, learn the dairy business, and then return to Greece. "However," he says, "I fell in love with the country, its people, and a girl." The two "funny animals" in the dairy department, the only woman and the foreign exchange student, found each other, married, and moved to Lena, Illinois, to work in the family cheese business.

The history of cheese in Lena began in 1925 when Fred Kolb founded the Kolb-Lena Cheese Company. At first he made specialty ethnic cheeses to be sold in the German markets of the Midwest. When Fred died in 1944, the brand name of Delico was adopted for all the company's cheeses. Fred's daughter, Freida, and her husband took over the reins. Freida, her own daughter, Dorothy, Dorothy's husband, Jim, and their four children and spouses expanded their markets until they were supplying the United States with a wide range of domestically produced specialty cheeses.

In December 1983, the Demeters opened a new plant gleaming with more than one million dollars' worth of modern equipment. Dorothy and Jim did not want to take such a big step unless they knew their children were committed to remain in the cheese business and carry on the tradition. Jim admits that perhaps they had brainwashed the kids a little, but it has worked.

Every day the new plant processes 250,000 pounds of milk into five or six different cheeses. Each type of cheese requires different curing and aging techniques, temperatures, and storage conditions. The biggest seller is Baby Swiss, a milder, softer, sweeter variety of Swiss cheese, developed in the early 1950s at Iowa State. Brie and Camembert, first made in the 1940s for the New York market, continue to be high-volume products for Kolb-Lena.

In the mid-1970s Jim Demeter, reaching back to his Greek heritage, began to produce Feta. Jim's Feta is a salty, semisoft cheese that is ripened in its own "milk juice" and can be kept almost indefinitely, if refrigerated. It is best if purchased in its own juices. It is available in a vacuum-packed form that should be stored in a jar or plastic container and covered with a brine made of three tablespoons of salt to a quart of water. This cheese was hardly known in America twenty years ago but is now extraordinarily popular and is often served in restaurants in a typical Greek salad. Traditionally, in Greece, Feta has been made of sheep's milk. Now most Feta in America and overseas is made from cow's milk; a different type of milk will be clearly stated on the label. The Demeters do make small quantities of Feta from a mixture of cow's and goat's milk, labeled as such.

Because of its dramatic growth in the eighties, Kolb-Lena became a prime acquisition target and was purchased by Zausner Foods in 1987. Jim and Dorothy, along with their two sons, Fred and Ted, stayed on with the new company. Then, in March of 1988, Jim and Dorothy were struck by a car while crossing a street in Florida. They survived the accident, fortunately, and as we go to press, they are planning to return to Kolb-Lena in the near future. This is good news for Kolb-Lena Cheese Company, and for all of us.

Chicken Breast with Feta and Olive Purée

Serves 4

Feta is a natural companion to olive purée. This rich paste made from olives and herbs is imported from the Mediterranean and is generally available in specialty outlets. If you are unable to find it, substitute your own mixture: pit Kalamata, Niçoise, or oil-cured olives and blend them to a paste in a food processor or blender with some good quality olive oil; add oregano and thyme to taste.

4 half chicken breasts, boned, skin intact
6 ounces Feta cheese, crumbled
2 tablespoons olive purée
1 or 2 garlic cloves, minced or pressed
1 teaspoon chopped fresh oregano
2 tablespoons butter
1 tablespoon olive oil
¼ cup dry white wine
4 Roma tomatoes, peeled, seeded, and chopped
1 tablespoon chopped fresh parsley
1 tablespoon chopped fresh chives

With your fingers, carefully form pockets in chicken breasts between skin and meat. Combine the Feta, olive purée, garlic, and oregano. Divide into 4 portions and stuff the mixture into the pockets under the skin of the chicken. Flatten and spread the stuffing to cover as much of the breast as possible.

Heat the butter and oil in a large skillet until sizzling. Add the chicken breasts, skin-side down. Cook over medium heat until the skin browns, about 4 to 5 minutes. Turn, and sauté for 4 to 5 minutes until cooked through. Remove the chicken from the pan and keep warm.

Pour off all but 1 tablespoon fat and return the skillet to the heat. Deglaze the pan by adding the wine and stirring to loosen any remaining bits. Add the tomatoes and simmer until most of the liquid is evaporated. Add the parsley and cook for 30 seconds. Serve the chicken breasts, sprinkled with chives, on a pool of tomato sauce.

The slow cooking of onions over low heat brings out their natural sugar while turning them a tantalizing color. In this beguiling combination of flavor and texture, onions complement the sweetness of pears and both are highlighted by sharp, salty Feta. The result is an exciting start to any meal.

  2 tablespoons butter
  2 large red onions, thinly sliced
  1 large or 2 small pears
  Half a lemon
  ¼ cup raspberry vinegar
  ½ cup walnut oil
  Salt and pepper to taste
  ½ pound fresh spinach, arugula, or watercress, washed and cut
    into a chiffonade
  4 ounces Feta cheese

Melt the butter in a medium skillet. Add the sliced onions and cook over low heat for 30 to 45 minutes, stirring occasionally. Set aside.

Peel and slice the pears. Squeeze lemon juice over them to prevent their browning.

Make a vinaigrette with the vinegar, oil, salt, and pepper. Toss the greens quickly in half of the vinaigrette.

Make a bed of greens on each of 4 salad plates. Place a quarter of the caramelized onions in the center of the greens. Surround the onions with pear slices. Crumble the cheese over the salad and drizzle with the remaining vinaigrette.

Pear and Caramelized Onion Salad

Serves 4

Kolb-Lena Cheese Company

Cucumber and Feta Salad

Serves 4

Ideal picnic fare or as an accompaniment to any hot and spicy grilled meat, this salad may be served cold or at room temperature. The first step, sweating the cucumber slices, draws out moisture that would otherwise dilute the Feta dressing.

1 large cucumber, peeled and thinly sliced
Salt
2 ounces Feta cheese, crumbled
4 tablespoons olive oil
1 tablespoon lemon juice
½ tablespoon chopped fresh dill
1 small garlic clove, diced
Generous grind of black pepper

Sprinkle the cucumber slices with salt. Allow them to sweat in a colander for 10 to 15 minutes and then dry them with paper towels. In a food processor or blender mix the remaining ingredients to make a dressing. Toss the cucumber slices with the dressing.

Tomato and Green Bean Ragout

Serves 4 to 6

Kolb-Lena Cheese Company

A richly flavored medley of summer produce, this accompaniment will embellish simply prepared meat or fish. Complete the meal with some crusty bread, a bottle of wine, and a dessert of fresh fruit.

4 large garlic cloves, minced
2 tablespoons olive oil
¾ pound tomatoes, peeled and coarsely chopped
1 pound green beans, cut into 1-inch pieces
Freshly ground black pepper, to taste
1 tablespoon fresh oregano
6 ounces Feta cheese, coarsely crumbled
Salt, to taste

In a large skillet, sauté the garlic in oil for 1 to 2 minutes, until softened. Add the tomatoes, beans, and black pepper. Cover and simmer until the beans are tender, approximately 10 minutes. If the tomatoes have rendered too much liquid, remove the cover for the last few minutes. Add the oregano and Feta and taste before adding salt. Heat until the cheese is just melted. Serve hot.

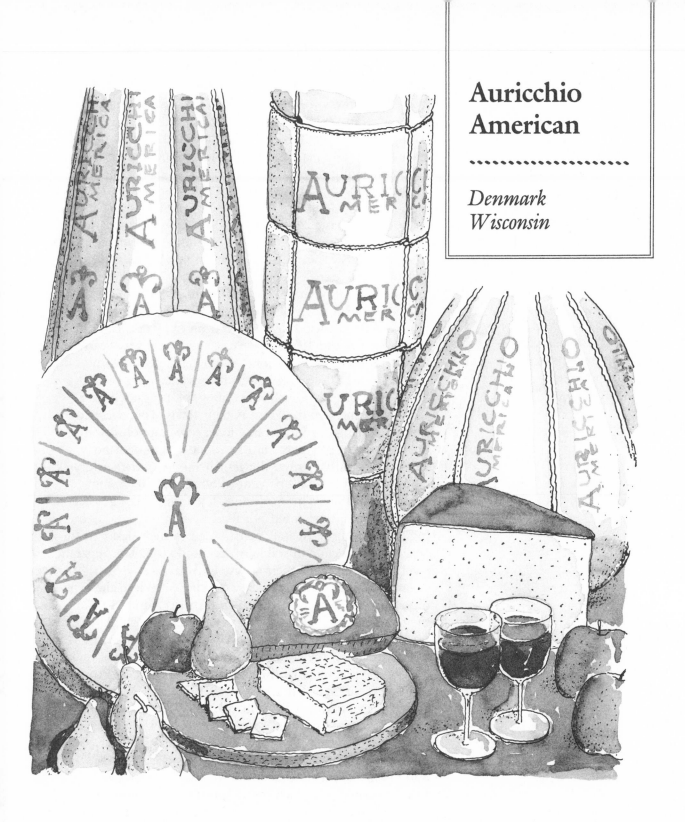

Auricchio
American

....

Denmark
Wisconsin

Auricchio
American

....

*Denmark
Wisconsin*

CHEESES: Aged Raw-milk
Provolone, Parmesan,
Romano, Asiago,
Fontina, Toscanello,
and Cold-Pack Cheese
RETAIL SALES: Yes
TOURS: Yes, by
appointment
MAIL ORDER: No

When you visualize an Italian delicatessen, what is the first image that enters your mind? Is it a vast array of odd shapes hanging from the ceiling? Do your eyes behold straw-wrapped bottles of Italian wine, braids and wreaths made of garlic, onion and peppers, dried salamis, and mammoth cheeses hanging by ropes? Our eyes are riveted to those remarkable cheeses, variously named Salame, Provole, Provolettine, Pear, and Mandarini. Such are the names of the assorted shapes of the basic cheese, Provolone. Closer examination often reveals the name Auricchio prominently stamped in red. This name has appeared on cheeses in our Italian/American delis for over four decades.

The Auricchio dynasty had its beginnings in the small northern Italian town of Cremona in 1877. It has taken four generations of Auricchios to perfect an old-world country recipe. By the late 1970s the Auricchio family was clearly the largest producer of Provolone in Italy and, possibly, the world. As the family story goes, they were sitting around a good piece of Provolone one evening, plotting their next step. The American market was their focus. They were cognizant of a change in American cheese consumption toward ethnic and specialty cheeses. Provolone was in demand. Americans clearly favored the Italian variety over their domestic version since 60 percent of what they ate was imported from Italy. The Auricchios knew that, because of U.S. import quotas, they could not increase their exports. Growing political unrest in Italy contributed to their desire to increase their revenue in stable American dollars. The apparent solution was to make their cheese in America.

Two members of the family were chosen to lead the expedition. In 1979, cousins Errico and Enrico Auricchio and their respective families arrived in the New World. After considerable investigation, they settled in Wisconsin because it is in the middle of the country and has an abundance of milk. To test the feasibility of their plan, they first decided to rent a cheese plant. When it appeared that all was well, they purchased their first plant in Denmark, Wisconsin. Despite all the care to start small and conservatively, they made their mistakes and at one point almost packed up and went home. The main difficulty was in marketing this cheese to the American public. To many consumers the word *imported* is magic and they will pay a much higher price for that premium. It is more difficult to get a good price for a domestic product even if it is of a higher quality than that of the local competition. The Auricchios were making cheese by the same techniques and using the same secret cultures as they did in Italy. How could that be communicated to the consumer?

Cheese marketing methods in America differ greatly from those in Italy. Obviously, Errico and Enrico needed help. That help came from Dan Carter, consultant to the cheese industry. Carter guided them to brokers, marketing networks, and trade shows and he provided promotional plans and package designs. More important, Errico hit the road promoting the cheese. He is a natural salesman: knowledgeable, charming, and debonair yet friendly and accessible. Perhaps his best asset is his delightfully infectious laugh.

Eventually, this high-quality cheese began to sell itself. At the time of our visit, the Denmark plant was processing a hundred thousand pounds of milk a day, for six days a week. That quantity has since doubled. Auricchio commands a higher price than do most other domestic Provolones because the public now associates the Auricchio label with higher quality. In 1982 an international jury confirmed the notion that Auricchio makes a superior product by awarding its domestic Provolone the title of the World's Best Provolone. According to Errico, the qualities that make this cheese better than the products of its competitors are a result of several cheese-making techniques. For example, in order to receive scrupulously clean and fresh milk, Auricchio's own delivery personnel collect it from their 150 suppliers each day. The cheese-making process does not include pasteurization, bleach, or preservatives. The Auricchios brought the bacterial culture and their particular knowledge of cheese making from Italy and, understandably, keep these secrets to themselves.

The cheese is essentially handmade. After a fairly basic curd-forming process, the resultant Mozzarellalike curd is cut and passed through hot water, which melts the curds together to form a large mass. At this point it is divided into which shapes the cheese will be formed. One variety is the sausage shape. By way of a special technique, five twenty-five-pound pieces of curd are molded into one 125-pound sausage shape. Three men are required to carry the embryonic Provolone to its stainless steel mold where its shape will be formed. Once formed, the hunk is soaked in a salt-water brine solution that ensures a salt content of between 1 and 1½ percent in the final product. The cheeses are waxed and hung by special cords sent from Italy in the temperature- and humidity-controlled aging rooms. Mild Provolone is aged for a minimum of sixty days; the sharper cheese is aged for at least seven months.

Pleased with the growth in sales of their Provolone, Errico and Enrico were motivated to expand. They found a second plant in Pulaski, Wisconsin, where they began to produce Parmesan, Romano, and Fontina. Enrico is particularly excited about their Fontina, which he believes will be the "Brie of the nineties." He is pleased, as well, with their Parmesan. He claims that the flavor of their domestic Parmesan is not the same as that of the *parmigiano-reggiano* from the Parma region of Italy, but that it is close. He attributes the comparable quality to Auricchio's techniques, of course, but also to the milk. In Parma, the cows are fed primarily on dry hay. Due to the long Midwestern winters, the cattle in Wisconsin are also primarily fed hay. Presently the Auricchios do not age their Parmesan as long as the cheese is typically aged in Italy. Errico points to the extra cost of aging cheese longer as the obstacle to effective competition with the imported variety. More and more he is being urged to produce a longer-aged domestic Parmesan. In his heart, Enrico is tempted but has not been convinced of the financial feasibility of such a project.

The Auricchios' entrance into America's domestic cheese market was timely, considering some current trends in American cheese consumption. Market studies predict that American cheese consumption will double by 1992. Sales of more flavorful specialty cheeses are increasing, as is the demand for products made in America. So, the next time you see those outlandish cheeses hanging in your favorite delicatessen, look carefully at the red stamp. It may well read, "Auricchio—American."

When we learned that one of the Auricchio family's favorite recipes is a cheese bread, we developed our version, a hearty meal in itself. Serve with a fresh green salad and a glass of wine.

Bread
¼ cup warm water
3 teaspoons honey
1 package active dry yeast (2½ teaspoons)
¾ cup milk, scalded and cooled to lukewarm
¼ cup butter, melted and cooled
1 egg, beaten
2 cups all-purpose flour
1 cup whole wheat flour

In a small bowl, mix the water, 1 teaspoon of the honey, and the yeast. Let sit for 10 minutes. Mix the milk, butter, the beaten egg, and the remaining 2 teaspoons honey into the yeast mixture. Add the flours and mix thoroughly, adding more flour if the dough is sticky. Knead until elastic, 5 to 7 minutes. Place the dough in an oiled bowl, cover, and let rise until doubled in bulk, 1½ to 2 hours.
   While the dough is rising, prepare the filling.

Filling
8 ounces Provolone, grated (2 cups)
8 ounces Fontina, grated (2 cups)
2½ ounces dried tomatoes, chopped (½ cup)
¼ cup pitted and chopped Niçoise olives
1 heaping tablespoon chopped fresh basil
2 eggs
¾ teaspoon freshly ground black pepper

Mix together both cheeses, the tomatoes, olives, basil, eggs, and pepper.

   When the dough has risen, roll it into a 15-inch-diameter circle. Pile the filling in the center. Bring up the edges of the dough, joining them in the center in a pinwheel fashion. Moisten the edges with water and pinch them closed. Place seam-up on a cornmeal-sprinkled baking pan. Let the bread rise for 30 to 45 minutes.
   Preheat the oven to 350°F. Bake for 1 hour in the preheated oven. Cool for 10 minutes before serving.

Auricchio Cheese Bread

Makes 1 large loaf

Auricchio American

Cheese- and Spinach- Stuffed Tomatoes

Serves 6

This savory accompaniment highlights simply grilled meats.

6 large vine-ripe tomatoes
1 bunch fresh spinach (approximately ⅓ pound), stems removed, washed, dried and coarsely chopped
8 ounces Ricotta
⅔ pound Fontina, grated (2⅔ cup)
2 ounces Parmesan, grated (¾ cup)
1 tablespoon capers
Freshly ground black pepper, to taste
½ cup chopped parsley
½ teaspoon anchovy paste or 1 anchovy fillet
2 garlic cloves, pressed

Preheat the oven to 400°F.

Submerge each tomato in boiling water for 1 minute. Cool in cold running water and peel. Cut off the top ½ inch and scoop out the pulp. Steam the spinach until just wilted. Drain well, squeezing out liquid. Mix with the three cheeses, capers, black pepper, parsley, anchovy, and garlic.

Divide the filling among the tomatoes and bake in the preheated oven until hot, approximately 5 minutes. Serve warm.

This recipe was inspired by a sumptuous truffle and cream-rich corn risotto created by Jerry DiVecchio, who is the Food Editor of Sunset magazine. We think the best accompaniment for this dish would be a simple, grilled lamb chop.

3 tablespoons butter
1 medium onion, coarsely chopped
2½ cups corn kernels, fresh or frozen
½ cup milk
½ cup heavy cream
Freshly ground black pepper
6 ounces Fontina, grated (1½ cups)
1 tablespoon chopped parsley

Melt the butter in a saucepan. Add the onion and cook over medium heat until soft but not brown. Add the corn. When the kernels are hot, add the milk, cream, and a generous grinding of black pepper. Increase the heat and cook until thickened, approximately 5 minutes. Cover and cook over low heat for 10 minutes. Add the cheese and stir over low heat until it has melted. Serve hot with a sprinkling of parsley.

Italian Creamy Corn

Serves 4

Auricchio American

Butternut Squash Risotto

Serves 6

There is nothing like a hearty and comforting risotto to warm those cold winter nights. Serve as a first course or with roasted meat.

¼ pound fresh, or 1 ounce dried, *shiitake* mushrooms
4 tablespoons butter
1 large onion, coarsely chopped
2 cups raw butternut squash, peeled and grated
1 cup Arborio rice
1½ to 2 cups rich chicken stock, heated and kept warm
1 cup Parmesan, grated (4 ounces)

If using dried *shiitake* mushrooms, soak them in hot water for 20 minutes. Drain and chop. Save the liquid for other uses. If using fresh mushrooms, simply wash and chop them.

Melt the butter in a heavy saucepan. Add the onion and sauté until soft. Add the mushrooms, squash, and rice. Gradually add the hot stock, ¼ cup at a time. Stir constantly over low heat until each addition is absorbed. Continue until the rice kernels are soft but still have a little crunch in the middle. Add the grated cheese. Stir until blended and melted. Serve hot.

Mozzarella Company

■-■-■-■-■-■-■-■-■-■

*Dallas
Texas*

Mozzarella Company

━━━━━━━━━━━━━━

Dallas
Texas

CHEESES: Mozzarella,
  Ricotta, Cream Cheese,
  Crème Fraîche, Texas
  Goat Cheese,
  Mascarpone, Scamorza,
  Caciotta, Herb
  Caciottas, Ancho Chile
  Caciotta, Taleggio, Feta
RETAIL SALES: Yes
TOURS: No
MAIL ORDER: Yes

"How many people get to have a job involving the two things they love most?" wondered Paula Lambert, the owner of the Mozzarella Company of Dallas, Texas. The two things she loves most, food and Italy, constitute her occupation. After graduating from college and teaching for a spell, Paula moved to Italy, where she remained for five years. While there, she was a regular customer at the lively and colorful marketplace. Ever present in her bag of groceries was her very favorite food, freshly made Mozzarella.

While in Italy, Paula met the man who was to become her husband, married him, and returned to America. From the moment they arrived, Paula was dedicated to a search for her favorite fresh cheese. But, alas, this search was to no avail. Though some importers had it flown here, it was already a few days old by the time she could obtain it. The cheese was simply not as she had remembered.

In 1981, Paula returned to Italy and, while there, decided she would make her own Mozzarella back home in Texas. She went to the cheese factory where her favorite cheese was made to learn the necessary skills from a second-generation cheese maker. Next, she found a cheese-making trade school in northern Italy and arranged to hire its most eminent professor to come to Texas during his summer vacation the following year. Her project in the works, the remaining details were, for Paula, a piece of cheesecake. Within six months of her return to Texas she had found two silent partners, remodeled an old building in a warehouse district of Dallas, bought her equipment and supplies, and hired two employees. When the Italian professor arrived, she was ready for him. He stayed a month to be certain that all the potential difficulties in the manufacturing process were addressed, and then she was on her own.

Now Paula could make fresh Mozzarella to her heart's content. Eventually, however, it became clear that it was not financially favorable to make only Mozzarella. The process involves much waiting for the curd to ripen. For Paula this was an irksome waste of time. The logical solution was to make Ricotta from the whey, which is exactly what she did. Within a year and a half of opening her factory, she was making not only Mozzarella and Ricotta but also Crème Fraîche. She then began selling flavored versions of her fresh Mozzarella, made by rolling out the Mozzarella into a big flat rectangle, covering it with prosciutto, dried tomatoes, or pesto, and then rolling it up jelly-roll fashion.

Still not satisfied that she and her assistants were fully employed, she returned to Italy, toured several factories, and learned to make some new cheeses, most notably Mascarpone and Caciotta, which differs from the Italian Cacciotta (a soft, delicate, buttery cheese) in that it is less soft and buttery and has a more bland taste. Once back in Texas, she added these, as well as a fresh Goat Cheese, to her already burgeoning line. The method for making Goat Cheese she divined herself. Her Goat Cheese is so popular that she sells almost as much of it as she does Mozzarella, her best seller.

At this point some local chefs contributed their own ideas to Paula's enterprise. Inspired by a growing pride in the regional cooking of Texas and the use of local ingredients, they urged her to make cheese with flavorings such as *ancho* chiles, garlic, and basil. This she did, most willingly.

As of this writing, Paula Lambert's Mozzarella Company offers more than twenty different cheeses. But one encounter with her is evidence enough that she is not stopping there. She is working on a Pecorino for which she is determinedly tracking down sheep's milk. This is no minor task in a country where sheep are not milked, but if anyone can make it happen, Paula can.

The Mozzarella Company has received much acclaim from local, state, and national press for its excellent cheeses. Paula's handmade, high-quality cheeses claim a unique position in Texas, where the populace is ready and eager for such products. Her Mozzarella is extraordinarily supple and softer in texture than are most handmade Mozzarellas we have tasted. For a traditionally bland cheese that is meant to be consumed very fresh, this Mozzarella definitely has flavor: sweet with pleasing acidic undertones.

Heeding her intuition and desires, Paula created a business in which she believes, providing herself with work that she likes. No thought had been directed toward acceptability of the product. No market research was attempted. It was merely a case of self-fulfillment that happened to occur in the right place at the right time.

Stuffed Squash Blossoms

Makes enough for approximately 30 medium-sized squash blossoms

Squash blossoms vary considerably in size, so it is impossible to give specific quantities for the stuffing. You must judge for yourself how much stuffing you will need, bearing in mind that the blossoms should be stuffed as full as possible. A medium-sized squash blossom will hold a one-inch cube of Mozzarella wrapped in half of a thin slice of prosciutto with one small basil leaf.

Stuffing variations
Goat Cheese, hot chile pepper, and cilantro
Goat Cheese, garlic slivers, and fresh thyme
Goat Cheese, chives, and olive purée (*see* page 154)
Goat Cheese or Mozzarella, dried tomato, and fresh basil
Mozzarella, prosciutto, and fresh basil
Mozzarella, anchovy fillet, and oregano

To stuff a blossom, hold the base with one hand while opening the petals wide enough with the other hand to insert the filling just to the point at which the petals divide. Twist the ends of the petals together gently.

Batter for 30 blossoms
1 cup all-purpose flour
1 cup beer

To ensure a crisp batter, mix the flour and beer, blend until smooth, and allow to rest for at least 1 hour.

Heat oil in a deep fryer or skillet to a temperature of 375°F. Dip the stuffed squash blossoms in batter to coat and drop them into the hot oil. Fry for 2 or 3 minutes, until lightly browned. Turn and repeat on the other side. Serve hot.

It is not absolutely necessary to grill the tomatoes for the sauce, but that extra step adds a dimension of smoky flavor that underscores the grilled eggplant.

1 large eggplant, sliced into ½-inch rounds
About 4 tablespoons olive oil
1 pound fresh tomatoes
1 small onion, chopped
2 garlic cloves, chopped
1 teaspoon fresh thyme
Salt and pepper to taste
1 pound fresh Mozzarella, sliced into ¼-inch-thick rounds
Parmesan or Dry Jack, grated, for garnish

Salt the sliced eggplant on both sides and place in a colander for 15 minutes. Wash and dry the slices and brush both sides with olive oil.

Place the tomatoes on a hot grill. Turn regularly until the skin is lightly blistered, 3 to 4 minutes. Cool, peel, and seed.

In a large skillet, heat 2 tablespoons olive oil, add the onion and garlic, and sauté gently until soft. Add the tomatoes, thyme, salt, and pepper. Simmer gently, for approximately 10 minutes.

Grill the eggplant for approximately 2 minutes on one side. Turn and place the slices of Mozzarella on the upturned, grilled side. Cook for approximately 2 minutes longer, until the eggplant is soft and the cheese melted.

On each of 4 serving plates make pyramids of eggplant by piling the smaller cheese-covered eggplant slices atop the larger ones. Cover the eggplant with grilled-tomato sauce and pass grated Parmesan.

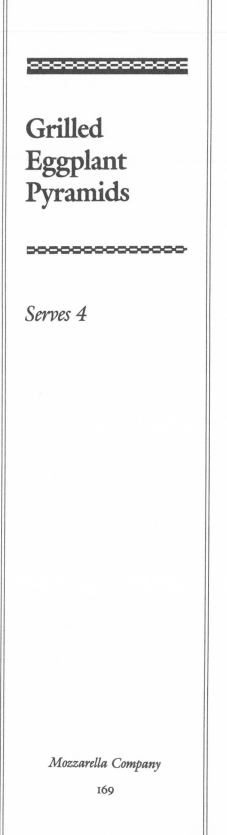

Grilled Eggplant Pyramids

Serves 4

Mozzarella Company

Tiramisu

Serves 8

A traditionally rich and light Italian dessert here assumes an American persona thanks to the substitution of American bourbon whiskey, American-made Mascarpone, and vanilla wafers for the usual Italian ingredients. It is as irresistible as the original.

24 ladyfingers or 30 vanilla wafers
⅓ cup bourbon whiskey
1 cup strong coffee
4 large eggs, separated
1 cup sugar
¾ pound Mascarpone
¾ ounce bittersweet chocolate, grated

Line the bottom and sides of a 2-quart baking dish with two-thirds of the ladyfingers or vanilla wafers.

Combine the bourbon and coffee. Sprinkle two-thirds of the coffee mixture over the ladyfingers in the dish. Beat the egg yolks with sugar until they are smooth and yellow. Add the Mascarpone and mix thoroughly. Beat the egg whites and fold in gently.

Pour half of the cheese mixture into the baking dish. Cover with the remaining ladyfingers or wafers. Sprinkle with the remaining coffee mixture. Top with half of the grated chocolate, then top with the remaining cheese mixture. Sprinkle on the remaining chocolate. Refrigerate for at least 2 hours.

Neither traditional for Mozzarella nor for Thailand, this recipe yields a salad that is fragrant, flavorful, colorful, and well worth any extra effort required to find the exotic ingredients.

4 tablespoons lime juice
3 tablespoons fish sauce*
4 garlic cloves, minced
2 stalks fresh lemon grass,* top ⅔ discarded, bottom, bulb-like 6 inches peeled and then sliced crosswise
½ pound Mozzarella, cut into 1-inch cubes
1 cup diced red onion
4 small Thai-style chiles,* or 1 *jalapeño,* seeded and minced
1 bunch leaf lettuce
1 cup cilantro leaves, loosely packed
4 tomatoes, sliced
½ cup peanuts, toasted in a 350°F oven for 5 to 6 minutes and chopped

In a food processor or blender, combine the lime juice, fish sauce, and garlic. Pour into a medium bowl. Add the diced lemon grass, cheese, onion, and chile. Marinate for at least 30 minutes.

Line a serving plate with lettuce leaves. Pile the cheese mixture in the center. Garnish with cilantro and tomatoes and sprinkle with peanuts.

*May be purchased in Thai or Asian markets.

Thai Mozzarella Salad

Serves 4

Mark Stech-Novak's Mozzarella Cakes

Serves 4

Mark Stech-Novak is a food consultant who creates mouth-watering recipes for restaurants in the San Francisco Bay Area. Fortunately, he was pleased to share this one with us.

2 ounces spinach, chopped, blanched, and squeezed dry
4 ounces Mozzarella, grated or shredded (1 cup)
3 ounces Ricotta
1 ounce pine nuts, toasted
2 tablespoons heavy cream
1 large egg
½ teaspoon white pepper
1 garlic clove, finely minced
½ cup dry, fine bread crumbs
½ cup semolina or unbleached white flour
Herb mixture (see recipe below)
4 tablespoons butter
1 large tomato, sliced into quarters
4 fresh basil leaves, cut into a chiffonade

Mix the spinach, cheeses, pine nuts, cream, egg, pepper, and garlic. Divide the mixture into 4 equal portions.

Mix together the crumbs, semolina, and ⅛ teaspoon of the herb mixture.

With floured hands, form the spinach mixture into patties approximately 3 inches in diameter. Coat with the crumb mixture and set aside.

Melt half of the butter in a nonstick skillet. Brown the cakes on one side, flip them over, and add the remaining butter. When the second side is brown, remove from the skillet and place on serving plates. Add the tomato slices to the skillet, sprinkle each with some of the remaining herb mixture, and sauté for approximately 30 seconds. Flip and sauté for another 30 seconds.

Place the tomato slices on the cakes and garnish with the basil. Serve immediately.

Herb mixture
¼ teaspoon dried tarragon
⅛ teaspoon anise seed
¼ teaspoon dried oregano
¼ teaspoon dried basil

Blend in a processor or grind with a mortar and pestle.

Tillamook County Creamery

⌇⌇⌇⌇⌇⌇⌇⌇⌇⌇⌇⌇⌇⌇⌇⌇

Tillamook
Oregon

CHEESES: Cheddar,
  Colby, Monterey Jack
RETAIL SALES: Yes
TOURS: Yes; view win-
  dow
MAIL ORDER: Yes

The northern Oregon coast has the perpetual green of a land blessed with moderate temperatures and abundant rainfall—a hundred inches of rain a year. Here the numerous streams and rivers cascade down forested hills, meander through lush grassy meadows and fields, and flow into the sea. No wonder the Indians of the area dubbed this verdant spot the "land of many waters" or *Tillamook.*

The first white settlers to arrive in this area were reminded of their native Switzerland. They knew that, with all that grass, they could raise dairy cows. Most of these dairymen turned the milk from their cows into butter. Some attempted to make cheese, producing an almost unpalatable species of Swiss cheese. Soon they were confronted with the problem of reaching the markets of Portland and San Francisco.

The roads from Tillamook to Portland consisted mainly of Indian trails that were clearly not suitable for the transportation of butter and cheese. The only vaguely reliable transportation was by boat. However, the boat schedule was subject to change and, if the weather were uncooperative, arrivals could be delayed for weeks. All the while, the Tillamook residents' cheese and butter suffered and, too often, spoiled. The farmers of the area, in an attempt to improve their predicament, cooperated to build their own boat. *Morningstar,* a sailing vessel, successfully solved their transport problem for a couple of years until it dumped itself on the Columbia River bar. Fortuitously, at around that time the railroad reached the coast.

By the late 1880s, it had become glaringly apparent that with the skim milk and buttermilk going to waste, the farmers needed to make something other than butter. The loose-knit group convinced Peter McIntosh, a cheese maker from Canada, to teach them to make Cheddar. Before the advent of McIntosh, the generally held notion was that good cheese could not be made in the area. The people blamed the weather, the grass, the ocean—anything rather than their lack of cheese-making skills—for their blown-up, bouncing cheeses. Peter McIntosh proved that good cheese could be made anywhere—if you knew how. Cheddar was chosen because it is a high-acid, rather dry cheese able to withstand abuse and will keep for a long time without refrigeration.

By the early 1900s, there were more than thirty cheese plants in Tillamook County. The typical small community consisted of a store, a school, and a cheese factory. At first,

Peter McIntosh operated his own factory and later was hired to operate several others. The McIntosh-influenced factories produced consistently high-quality cheese but most of the others did not. Consumers in the big cities began to demand some consistency in the cheese they were buying from the coastal areas.

Carl Haberlach, an attorney and cheese broker newly arrived from Portland, convinced individual producers and small cooperatives to join together. In 1909 they formed the Tillamook Co-operative Creameries Association in an attempt to centralize their marketing efforts. This was a good beginning but did not solve the problem of inconsistent cheeses. So, the battle began. While many members recognized the need for production standards, others resisted. Farmers and cheese makers are an independent breed, each choosing his occupation in order to be his own "big cheese." This co-op business smacked too much of some Portland city slicker's telling them what to do. Eventually, however, reason and economics prevailed and standards were developed.

Between 1917 and 1918 the Tillamook Co-operative Creameries Association became the first cooperative cheese producer to develop a brand name. The name "Tillamook" was chosen as the identifying label for the cheeses made by the cooperating cheese plants. Before long, because consumers began to equate Tillamook with high-quality Cheddar, consistency of quality became more important than ever. The Tillamook Co-op considered consistency its primary goal, then as now.

Co-op members came to realize that, in order to produce a consistently high-quality cheese, they must provide the highest quality milk. Unlike most other co-op cheese factories, Tillamook does not work for the farmers, and is therefore not required to accept all the milk that is delivered, regardless of quality. Tillamook cheese sells for a higher price than do most other Cheddars, which enables the co-op to pay a higher price for its milk, and hence to demand the best possible milk.

We spoke with Harold Schield, Tillamook's assistant general manager, who is representative of the "old school" Tillamook employee. Harold grew up on a small dairy in Tillamook County and began working in the packaging department of the cheese factory in 1958. Since then he has worked in almost every aspect of the factory operation. The "new school" of factory employees come from everywhere, are unionized, and have very little history in the dairy business. Times have changed.

Today, the large, centralized Tillamook cheese factory, one of two remaining Cheddar facilities along the Oregon coast, processes one million pounds of milk a day, seven days a week. On one of the most scenic highways in America, Tillamook welcomes over six hundred thousand visitors a year in a large visitor center. Despite the immense capacity of the plant and the sophistication of the cheese-making process at Tillamook, there remains a considerable amount of hands-on work to be done. The milk is heated and cultured. The resultant curds are cut, then drained of whey in large vats. Through the large plate-glass window of the visitor center, one views numerous employees hustling and bustling, engaged in various phases of their cheese-making activities. Tillamook is quite unlike most large cheese production plants these days, that are computerized and require scant human presence.

We asked Harold Schield what makes Tillamook Cheddar different from other Cheddars. His immediate response was that it is different because it is superior. He feels that their Cheddar is the best because the milk supply is the best. Extra aging time also contributes to its superiority in providing a deeper, more concentrated flavor. And Tillamook's consistency, the achievement of a long-cherished goal, assures the consumer of a recognizable texture and flavor. With unexpected candor, Harold admits that perhaps their attention to consistency prevents them from making that occasional outstanding cheese. However, this same consistency guards against the occasional wretched cheese. Our favorite, the Tillamook Proprietor's Reserve Cheddar, aged for at least twenty-four months, stands with the best of America's Cheddars. Distinct from Vermont and New York white Cheddars in its smoother texture and yellow color, the flavor is complex, sweet, and delicious.

Tillamook's name is legend on the West Coast. The cheese is sold in supermarket chains in California, Oregon, Washington, Phoenix, Salt Lake, and Denver. Those who live elsewhere may discover it in specialty cheese stores or order it directly from the plant. Best yet, when you next drive along the Oregon coast, stop at the Tillamook cheese factory and get it from the source.

Tillamook County, in the northwest corner of Oregon, produces an array of fruit, vegetables, and seafood. This recipe celebrates that abundance. When tomatoes are in season, slice them thickly, sprinkle with olive oil, black pepper, and parsley and serve with this pie.

½ pound sharp Cheddar
½ cup butter
1 cup all-purpose flour
3 to 5 tablespoons ice water
3 eggs, beaten
¾ cup heavy cream
1 cup peas, fresh or frozen
1 cup green onion, diced
1½ cups corn kernels, fresh or frozen
6 ounces fresh salmon, boned and cut into 1-inch pieces

Grate 3 ounces of the Cheddar, which will yield ¾ cup, and cut the rest into ½-inch cubes. Mix the butter, flour, and the grated cheese in a food processor or with a pastry blender until crumbly. Add enough ice water to form a dough. Cover and chill for at least 30 minutes.

Preheat the oven to 400°F. Roll out the dough and line a deep, 9-inch pie pan. Fill with pie weights. Bake the shell in the preheated oven for 8 minutes. Remove from the oven.

Make the filling by mixing the eggs and cream and folding in the cheese, vegetables, and salmon. Pour the mixture into the pie shell. Bake in the preheated oven for 20 to 25 minutes, until set and lightly browned. Serve hot or at room temperature.

Tillamook County Pie

Serves 6 to 8

Tillamook County Creamery

Black Bean Tostada

Serves 6

Black or turtle beans, a staple of Central and South America, are grown in the southern United States and traditionally used in soups. Here, the hearty black-bean flavor is enhanced by the interesting smokiness of *chipotle* peppers. These smoke-roasted jalapeños *are sold in cans in the Mexican food section of many supermarkets. Puréed with a light vegetable oil, they are easier to use.*

Vinaigrette
½ cup corn oil
Juice of 1 lime
2 garlic cloves, minced
2 teaspoons puréed *chipotle* peppers
2 teaspoons cumin seed, freshly crushed
1½ teaspoons minced fresh oregano
½ teaspoon salt
Generous grind black pepper
¼ teaspoon chili powder
⅛ teaspoon cayenne pepper

Combine all ingredients in a blender or food processor. Set aside.

Black Bean Salad
4 ounces Cheddar
3 cups cooked black beans
1 cup corn kernels, parboiled
1 medium tomato, diced
½ cup green onions, thinly sliced
¼ cup cilantro leaves, coarsely chopped

Dice the Cheddar into pieces the size of the corn kernels. In a medium bowl, combine all the ingredients. Toss with the vinaigrette.

Tostadas
Cooking oil
6 blue or yellow corn tortillas
Head of leaf lettuce, washed, dried, and cut into a chiffonade
½ cup cilantro leaves, chopped

Heat half an inch of cooking oil in a small skillet over medium heat until hot but not smoking. Fry one tortilla at a time, turning once to crisp thoroughly. Drain on paper towels.

To assemble the tostadas, place one crisp tortilla on each of 6 plates. Cover the tortillas with the lettuce *chiffonade*. Divide the bean salad evenly among the 6 tostadas. Garnish with cilantro.

A dynamic combination of smoke, sweet, spice, and cheese, these sandwiches will be gobbled up immediately. Serve with cold beer.

Mayonnaise
8 slices rye bread, toasted
4 handfuls arugula, watercress, spinach, or a combination of these greens
1 cup mango or peach chutney
6 ounces smoked turkey, thinly sliced
6 ounces sharp Cheddar, thinly sliced

Spread mayonnaise to taste on toasted bread. Arrange the greens on four of the slices of bread. Top with chutney. Divide the turkey and Cheddar into 4 equal portions. Place the portions of turkey onto a heatproof dish and top each with Cheddar. Heat briefly in a 400°F oven or microwave oven until the cheese is just melted. Arrange on top of the chutney. Cover with the remaining slices of bread. Cut each sandwich in half and serve.

Smoked Turkey and Chutney Sandwiches

Serves 4

Tillamook County Creamery

Cheddar and Oyster Pot-Pie

Serves 4

The Pacific Northwest is as famous for its oysters as it is for its Cheddar. This recipe combines the two in a sumptuously rich preparation that you will want to make again and again. Serve with a crisp green salad and a tart, high-acid white wine from Oregon or Washington.

³/₄ cup butter
1¼ cups all-purpose flour
¼ teaspoon salt
³/₄ tablespoon ice water
1 medium red onion, diced
1 pound unpeeled white potatoes, cut in ½-inch cubes
1 cup milk
½ cup heavy cream
¼ cup sherry
6 ounces sharp Cheddar, grated (1⅓ cups)
10 ounces fresh oysters

In a food processor or with pastry blender, mix ½ cup of the butter with the flour and salt until pea-sized. Gradually add water to form a ball. Cover and chill for at least 30 minutes.

In a medium saucepan melt the remaining ¼ cup butter. Add the onion and potato, cover, and cook over medium heat until the potatoes are slightly softened, approximately 10 minutes. Add the milk and cream. Increase the heat to medium-high and simmer until the mixture has thickened and the potatoes are tender, approximately 10 minutes. Lower the heat and add the sherry and Cheddar, stirring until the cheese is melted.

Preheat the oven to 425°F. Cut the pastry into 4 equal sections. Roll out 4 rounds, each large enough to cover a 12-ounce ramekin. Lightly butter 4 ramekins and distribute the oysters equally among them. (If the oysters are large, cut them in half or in quarters.) Pour in the potato and cheese mixture to cover the oysters, filling the ramekins to within ½ an inch of the top. Cover each ramekin with a pastry round. Seal, flute, and vent each crust topping. Bake in the preheated oven for 12 to 15 minutes, until the crust is brown and the filling bubbly.

Tillamook County Creamery

Stirring in the culture to set Nancy's Rennetless Cottage Cheese

Nancy's of Oregon

························

Eugene
Oregon

CHEESES: Cream Cheese
   and Cottage Cheese
RETAIL SALES: Yes
TOURS: No
MAIL ORDER: No

It was Nancy's unusually delectable, rich, soft Cream Cheese that lured us to Springfield, Oregon, just south of the university town of Eugene. The flavors of this elegant concoction are pure and true. It is a most original Cream Cheese formulated by a most unusual group of people. Springfield Dairy is owned and managed by Chuck and Sue Kesey, members of a noted Oregonian family. Chuck's brother, Ken, is a renowned author. Their father was a creamery manager, a mover and shaker in his chosen field. Chuck, himself, is the creative force behind Nancy's.

In 1960, having spent his entire life working in the creamery with his father, Chuck graduated from Oregon University with a degree in dairy technology. It was a time of change in the Oregon dairy industry, the big plants having recently switched from bottling milk in glass to filling cartons. Yet many consumers still preferred their milk in glass bottles. Dairygold, the large creamery managed by Chuck's father, had purchased a tiny ice cream plant, idle since 1956, which Chuck's father offered to him and his new wife, Sue, to run as a glass-bottling facility.

After nine years of hard work, little profit, and minimal satisfaction, Chuck, an inveterate tinkerer and researcher, announced that he wanted to make cultured products. They had no idea how to make yogurt, so they experimented until they created a product that pleased them. Nancy Hamren, then a new employee, proved to be instrumental in the development of the style of the product, hence the name, Nancy's. As fortune would have it, Nancy's Honey Yogurt appeared just as the natural foods industry was coming into its own. Nancy's found a niche in that segment of the market and simply flowed with the rising tide.

About 90 percent of Nancy's production and business is yogurt. Other products are fluid *kefir* (a cultured drink), sour cream, Cottage Cheese, and Cream Cheese. As the offerings have expanded from the original yogurt, the one guiding credo has been to make each item match the quality of the yogurt. Thus, each new product has been subject to careful consideration, thorough research, and repeated experimentation.

Both for flavor and because it promotes good health, all of Nancy's products contain *Acidophilus,* a bacteria that alters the microbial flora of the intestinal tract. The Cottage and Cream Cheeses are made with some old-fashioned methods and some new, unorthodox ones. The Cottage Cheese, unlike most commercial Cottage Cheese, contains no rennet. It is made with a lactic culture that is left overnight to set. In the morning, the cheese is cut, then cooked in the whey. Apparently in large, commercial plants the whey is drained off and the curds cooked in water for a more bland flavor. Nancy's process takes forty-eight hours to guide the milk from set to package; the "big guys" complete this process in a mere eight hours. Perhaps it is the extra time taken at Nancy's that creates a flavor reminiscent of the Cottage Cheese that used to be made on local farms. Nancy's Cottage Cheese differs from the standard variety that we are used to in that it has a tangier, more acid taste, less salt, and a texture that is denser and more uneven. Most commonly available Cottage Cheeses have more "curd and cream differentiation"—that is, the curds are more pronounced and there is more liquid—making it a "lighter" product.

The cheese maker who taught them to make Cottage Cheese shared his special secret, he could tell that the cheese was ready when the curd felt like the inside of a lady's thigh. After the cheese is cooked to perfection, the whey is drained and the curds rinsed twice with cold water. A mixture of milk and cream is added to the curds to raise the butterfat level to 4 percent and to adjust the moisture. The cheese is very lightly salted. Sue claims that, "We get away with so little salt because there is already so much flavor in our cheese."

Their Cream Cheese, too, is not of the textbook variety. Soft and spreadable, it comes in a cup. An unusual two-stage culturing system is employed. First an *Acidophilus* culture is introduced when the milk and cream mixture has cooled after being pasteurized. It is allowed to cool further, then is inoculated with a lactic culture and packaged. The cheese incubates in the cups in which it is sold. Again, as with the Cottage Cheese, no rennet is added.

We visited the old, small creamery where Nancy's received eighty-five thousand pounds of milk each week from a three-county area, delivered through a farmers' co-op. Now Chuck and Sue are happily ensconced in Eugene, in a larger facility that they have been readying for years. Some time ago, they bought a twenty-five-year-old meat-processing plant, which they have gradually remodeled, while looking forward to the day they could move out of their cramped quarters. Sue explains, "We are not risk takers. We move slowly."

Bright, friendly, and accessible, Sue Kesey is the person who makes Nancy's run. Her boundless energy drives the twenty full- and part-time employees who comprise her work force, while she answers the telephone, devises the schedules, and solves numerous daily problems. Sue does not hide her unswerving respect and admiration for her husband. She proudly describes Chuck as a "great creative mind that is innovative and a bit askew." His role in their business is that of a guardian angel and a guiding light. His expertise is drawn upon for the smooth operation of the building and equipment. It is Chuck who thinks about the future and, in that sense, he deals largely with the conceptual aspects of the business.

Nancy, the donator of the company's name, remains an integral part of the business. She works as the head bookkeeper but she is also respected and valued for her contributions toward product development. This attractive woman has a quiet self-assured manner, bright eyes, and a sense of humor. She and Sue work well together, and it is apparent she is a "member of the family."

Originally the natural foods industry was the marketing arm of Nancy's. It remains a vital part of their business and Sue is loyal to the distributors with whom she has worked closely since the early 1970s. Though the natural foods business has grown considerably since then, it can no longer be an exclusive funnel for Nancy's growing line of products, which are now also available in supermarkets.

The creamery business provides Sue and Chuck with sustenance for their souls as well as their pocketbooks. Sue comments, "Milk is such a great medium and Chuck is such a great experimenter." They enjoy working with milk as they do now and feel fortunate, blessed by fate, that their timing was right. But there is more to the success of Nancy's than an appreciation for milk and mere chance. There is hard work. Sue fixed us with her intense eyes and said, "When you own your own business, it's 100 percent. There's no off. You are always on." Then she smiled, "I like working. I like what I'm doing."

Though some of the most intensely flavored berries we have tasted were grown in Oregon, these tarts are wonderful made with any ripe berries, grown anywhere. We recommend that you have the tart shells baked, the berries macerated, and the cheese mixture prepared. Then assemble the tarts just before serving.

1 cup all-purpose flour
½ cup butter
⅓ cup sugar
1 pint strawberries
2 to 4 tablespoons orange-flavored liqueur
1 egg white
3 tablespoons sugar
¼ teaspoon vanilla extract
8 ounces Cream Cheese
½ pint raspberries
Fresh mint sprigs, for garnish

Thoroughly mix the flour, butter, and sugar by hand or in a food processor. Form into a ball and chill for at least 1 hour.

Preheat the oven to 375°F. Divide the dough into 6 equal portions and press into individual, 3-inch tart pans. Bake for 15 minutes in the preheated oven, until lightly browned. Cool thoroughly.

Slice the strawberries, sprinkle with orange liqueur, and allow them to soak for 30 minutes.

Whip the egg white until it is stiff. Add the sugar and vanilla to the Cream Cheese. Gently fold the Cream Cheese into the egg white.

Arrange the strawberry slices in the tart shells. Arrange half of the raspberries over the strawberries. Smooth the cheese mixture over the berries. Arrange the remaining raspberries on top of the cheese. Garnish with mint sprigs and serve.

Oregon Berry Tarts

Serves 6

Nancy's of Oregon

Nanny's Kugel

Serves 8 to 10

Actually, Nanny never made it like this, but her kugel provided the inspiration for this updated version. Serve in three-inch squares to accompany vegetable stews or braised meats.

6 eggs, beaten
3 cups milk
1 cup Cottage Cheese
1 cup Parmesan, grated
1 cup sour cream
1/4 teaspoon chopped fresh rosemary leaves
4 garlic cloves, pressed
1 teaspoon salt
Freshly ground black pepper, to taste
12 ounces wide egg noodles
1/2 cup butter

Preheat the oven to 350°F.

Mix together the eggs, milk, cheeses, sour cream, rosemary, garlic, salt, and pepper in a large bowl.

Cook the noodles al dente. Drain well and add to the egg mixture.

Pour into a buttered 9-by-13-inch baking pan. Dot with the remaining butter. Bake in the preheated oven for 20 to 25 minutes, until set and the top is lightly browned. Serve hot.

Thanks again to Michael Clark for another unusual contribution! Michael's Cheesecake is delectable, but be warned that it requires several hours to firm. We suggest you make it at least twelve hours before you plan to serve it.

Crust
1½ cups graham cracker crumbs
½ cup butter
1 teaspoon sugar
1 teaspoon cinnamon

Combine all the ingredients and press into a 9-inch springform pan.

Filling
2 pounds Cream Cheese, at room temperature
1 cup sugar
3 eggs
½ cup butter, melted and cooled
1 bottle (750 ml) Muscat Canelli wine

Preheat the oven to 375°F. Combine the Cream Cheese and sugar. Add the eggs, one at a time. Blend in the butter and the wine. Pour into the springform pan. Bake in the preheated oven for 60 to 75 minutes, until browned.

The cheesecake will still be somewhat liquid. Allow to cool thoroughly, preferably overnight, before serving. Do not refrigerate.

Michael's Cheesecake

Serves 10

Nancy's of Oregon

Spinach and Smoked Clam Turnovers

■■■■■■■■■■■■■■■■■■■■■■■■■

••••••••••••••••••••••

Makes 18 turnovers

These first-course turnovers are crowd pleasers as snacks for your soccer team's celebration or as food for thought during your monthly book club meeting.

1 package frozen puff pastry
2 cups Cottage Cheese
1 egg, beaten
2 bunches fresh spinach, washed, steamed, drained, and chopped
¼ cup minced shallots
1 tin (4 ounces) smoked baby clams or oysters
½ teaspoon salt
Freshly ground black pepper

Defrost the puff pastry.

Meanwhile, drain the Cottage Cheese in a sieve over a bowl for at least 30 minutes. Mix the egg with the drained Cottage Cheese and add the chopped spinach, shallots, clams, salt, and pepper.

Preheat the oven to 400°F. Roll each pastry sheet out into a square measuring approximately 15 inches. Cut each sheet into 9 equal squares, each measuring approximately 3½ inches.

Divide the spinach mixture evenly among the squares, placing a dollop in the center of each. Fold the pastry to form triangles. Seal by moistening the edges with water and crimping them with the tines of a fork.

Place on a cookie sheet and bake in the preheated oven for approximately 20 to 25 minutes, until puffed and golden brown. Serve while hot and crisp.

Rogue River Valley Creamery

◼━◼━◼━◼━◼━◼━◼━◼━◼

*Central Point
Oregon*

CHEESES: Blue, Cheddar,
  Raw-milk Cheddar,
  Monterey Jack,
  Mozzarella
RETAIL SALES: Yes
TOURS: By appointment
MAIL ORDER: Yes

On a foggy morning in Central Point, Oregon, we met Thomas G. Vella. As we grew accustomed to his odd, raspy whisper, we were enchanted by his sharp humor and world view. His bright eyes danced and he smiled at us as he spoke. We had to smile, too. This lovable old geezer seemed pleased at the prospect of an interview by two admiring women. He knew how to charm us, and so the story unraveled.

In 1934, at a time when small, independent cheese plants usually contracted to produce cheese for large companies such as Kraft, Thomas Vèlla did just that in Sonoma, California. Searching for small plants to purchase, Kraft's West Coast buyer made several forays into the Northwest, a region attractive because of the high-quality Cheddar produced in Tillamook. He came upon a facility in Central Point that, despite support from the city in the form of donated land and financing, was stumbling along and producing a rather inferior Cheddar.

The buyer convinced Thomas to take the train to Oregon and look at the factory. Savvy young Thomas was a risk taker and, as a man who loved a challenge, he relished the prospect of tackling the project. He made a deal with Kraft: if he could elevate the quality of the cheese produced in the plant, they would buy all the cheese he could produce there. They signed a six-month trial agreement.

Vella was convinced that war was imminent and food supplies would be important. He felt it was necessary to secure and expand control of the southern Oregon milk supply. To accomplish this, Vella bought cows for the dairymen of southern Oregon. This purchase they repaid through deductions from their milk checks over the following months. Just before the outbreak of the war, Vella had secured 380 patrons and owed Kraft a whopping $400,000 for financing his project. Within two years Vella had completely repaid his debt to Kraft. His little factory in Central Point managed to push out five million pounds of Cheddar toward the war effort. After the war, the management of Kraft joined Borden and Vella followed their lead. He converted his Central Point facility to become the first plant in Oregon to produce Cottage Cheese. In the fifties Vella's cheese empire experienced a boom that was to last into the eighties.

In 1956, Thomas traveled with his wife to Roquefort, France. He knew something about the way in which Gorgonzola, one of his favorite cheeses, was made and he wanted to add to that knowledge. He became fast friends with the Italian superintendent at the Roquefort plant. He returned to Central Point in 1957 to build an addition to the plant to house his Oregon Blue Cheese operation.

Soon Vella was producing twenty thousand five- to six-pound wheels of Blue Cheese each month and employing about a dozen people in order to do so. He sold 90 percent of the production to Borden and the rest under his own label. It was a busy, fruitful time for Thomas Vella. He was energetic enough to not be fazed by his regular train travel as he divided his time between California, where he was still managing the Sonoma plant, and Oregon. Nor could he have known then that he would continue this routine for forty years. He was young and could take on the world.

In the late sixties, he began producing Cheddar again. Following his bent toward specialty products, he chose to make a white raw-milk Cheddar, which he aged and then sold to the newly flourishing Northwest health-food market. Eventually, he stopped selling cheese to Borden, and stopped making Cottage Cheese altogether, having discovered an apparently endless demand for his delicious Cheddar.

Today the plant at Central Point produces Blue Cheese, Monterey Jack, and raw-milk and pasteurized Cheddar. In the bloom of his youth, his plant operated for five days a week, receiving between fifty and sixty thousand pounds of milk a day. However, today, it is running at a more leisurely rate—the milk is delivered only three or four days a week—a schedule more fitting for a man who, though carrying the spark and energy of his youth, has had to slow his pace somewhat.

Perhaps some of the original 380 patrons still sell their milk to Vella, but, if so, it is under the auspices of their co-op. Times have changed, but Oregon's milk continues to be of exemplary quality. Vella attributes this to the lush pastures the cows, unlike their California cousins, enjoy throughout the summer. Also, he believes that, because the nights are always cool, the cows rest better and this is favorable to the production of good milk.

As it happened, we visited the plant on a day when no cheese was being made. In its quiet beauty, the old railroad-flanked building felt as if it were a part of history. The shining equipment reflected the sunlight filtering softly into the tiled rooms through the opaque glass of the windows. It was spotless and orderly, yet from the rooms of this labyrinthine building emanated an indescribable warmth and coziness. We could imagine it filled with the bustle of cheese makers, machinery, and milk. Nor, that day, was milk being converted to cheese in the separate facility next door where the Blue Cheese is made. However, the large aging rooms were filled with aromatic wheels of cheese at different stages of maturity. Because of its unique microbiology and its labor-intensive process, it is essential that this cheese is manufactured in a separate location. This extra requirement, along with the handwork involved from start to finish (including a month during which each cheese is handled daily), makes Blue Cheese comparatively costly.

Presently approximately 70 percent of the plant's output is Cheddar and Jack, 20 percent is Blue, and 10 percent fresh, handmade Mozzarella, which is sold to local restaurants. Though law requires that raw-milk Cheddar be aged for sixty days, Vella nurtures extra flavor with an additional sixty days of aging. Similarly, he holds the Blue Cheese for thirty days beyond the traditional ninety. It is sold through distributors, mainly on the West Coast and as far east as Denver. The locals keep the business in the tiny factory store moving at a brisk pace.

Our eighty-eight-year-old host, as befits his experience and sagacity, willingly shared his memories, opinions, and advice. He nostalgically recalled the days when cheese makers shared their problems, expertise, and even bought equipment collectively. He bemoaned changes in the dairies, now that cows are no longer pastured as they were in times past. Though the milk is of high quality, the taste is not the same. He pondered the absurdity of pushing cows to produce when, in fact, there is a milk surplus, and the milk has less flavor. It has become much more difficult for the cheese maker to make flavorful cheese.

Thomas Vella has always loved making cheese. He believes that one must love it because it is not a business from which one is likely to get rich. He allowed that, perhaps, if a small plant produces four or five varieties of cheese, one could possibly make it profitable these days. But he has witnessed the demise of innumerable small plants over the years and observed the growth of the super-large cheese companies. The only hope for the small-scale cheese maker is to sell a product that is different, a specialty product unlike any other.

Knowing that Thomas was approaching the end of his career, we were pleased to learn the destiny of this wonderful cheese factory. Thomas's son, Ignazio, thirty years his junior, who has turned the Sonoma plant into a prosperous concern, is ready to manage the Oregon plant. Meanwhile, Ignazio's daughter, Elena, who is known as Chickie, is working with him in Sonoma and being groomed to take over the management of that facility when her father goes to Oregon. It is comforting to know that such a strong pride in family, tradition, and continuity exists here.

Rogue River Valley Creamery

Apple, Watercress, and Blue Cheese Salad

Serves 4 to 6

Bright, crunchy, and simple, this salad will catch your attention with its combination of sweet, salty, and peppery flavors. You will want to serve it again and again.

2 large pippin apples, cored
4 ounces Blue Cheese
2 cups watercress leaves, loosely packed
1 cup cashews, toasted
½ cup walnut oil
¼ cup raspberry vinegar

Cut the apples into eighths and then the wedges in half. Crumble the Blue Cheese into large pieces. Place the watercress, apples, cashews, and Blue Cheese in a serving bowl. Mix the oil and vinegar, pour over the other ingredients, mix lightly and serve immediately.

What a delightful way to start the day! Very different from the usual breakfast fare, this savory preparation is easy, quick, and nutritious. The asparagus, eggs, and white sauce can all be prepared in advance. If refrigerated, the asparagus and eggs should be brought to room temperature; the white sauce should be heated.

2 thick slices whole wheat bread
6 medium asparagus spears, steamed and cooled
2 hard-boiled eggs
1 ounce Blue Cheese, crumbled
1 tablespoon chopped chives
White sauce (recipe follows)

Lightly toast the bread and place on serving plates. Slice the eggs into rounds and arrange on the toast. Place the asparagus over the eggs. Crumble the cheese over the asparagus. Top with white sauce and sprinkle with chives. Serve immediately.

White Sauce
1 large shallot, minced
2 tablespoons unsalted butter
2 tablespoons all-purpose flour
1 cup milk, warmed
Salt and pepper

In small, heavy saucepan, sauté the shallot in butter until soft. Add the flour. Cook over low heat for 2 minutes, stirring. Gradually add the milk, stirring constantly, until the sauce has thickened. Salt and pepper to taste.

Blue Morning

Serves 2

Rogue River Valley Creamery

Blue
Note
Crackers

Makes about 36 crackers

Great little munchies for apéritif time! Keep some of this dough on hand in the freezer for last-minute entertaining.

½ pound white Cheddar, grated (2 cups)
2 ounces Blue Cheese, crumbled (½ cup)
1 cup all-purpose flour
½ cup unsalted butter
1 teaspoon sugar
½ teaspoon salt

Mix all the ingredients in a food processor or by hand until well blended and a ball forms. Chill for at least 30 minutes.

Preheat the oven to 375°F. Roll the dough out to a thickness of ¼ inch and, with a cookie cutter or shot glass, cut into rounds about 1½ to 2 inches in diameter. Bake on a lightly greased cookie sheet for 15 minutes in the preheated oven. Overcooking turns them bitter.

Rogue River Valley Creamery

Oregon Blue Cheese teams up with raspberries to provide an unbeatable combination. Brighten up your everyday dinner salad with this novel twist.

    1 bunch fresh spinach, stemmed, washed, and dried
    3 ounces Blue Cheese, crumbled
    1 cup fresh raspberries
    2 tablespoons raspberry vinegar
    4 tablespoons walnut or olive oil
    ¾ teaspoon Dijon mustard
    Generous grind of black pepper
    ¼ teaspoon salt

Arrange the spinach on a serving platter. Top with the cheese and raspberries. Combine the vinegar, oil, mustard, black pepper, and salt. Drizzle on the salad.

Blue Raspberry Salad

Serves 4

Baked Stuffed Onions

Serves 4

A happy combination of two Vella cheeses fills these onions. Serve them as a first course with sliced, toasted French bread croutons, or as part of a festive holiday meal.

4 medium onions
1 to 2 ounces Blue Cheese, crumbled (¼ to ½ cup)
4 ounces Jack, grated (1 cup)
¾ teaspoon fresh thyme
2 tablespoons butter
¼ cup fine bread crumbs

Preheat the oven to 400°F.

Bake the unpeeled onions for 1 hour. Remove and cool enough to handle. Increase the oven heat to 500°F. Peel the onions and cut a slice, approximately ½-inch thick, from one end of each. Squeeze or scoop out the inner part, leaving at least half an inch of shell.

Thoroughly chop half the reserved inner part of the onions and mix it well with the cheeses, ½ teaspoon fresh thyme, and 1 tablespoon of the butter. Stuff the onion shells with the cheese mixture.

Combine the remaining tablespoon butter with the bread crumbs and the remaining ¼ teaspoon thyme and dot this mixture over the tops of the stuffed onions.

Cook in the preheated oven for 2 to 4 minutes, or until the onions are heated through and the tops slightly browned. Serve immediately.

Inspecting vats of finished Bocconcini

Italcheese, Inc.

▗▄▄▄▄▄▄▄▄▄▄▄▄▄▄▄▄▄▄▄

*Gardena
California*

CHEESES: Ricotta, Moz-
    zarella, Bocconcini,
    Smoked Mozzarella,
    and Mascarpone
RETAIL SALES: No
TOURS: Yes
MAIL ORDER: No

When Virgil Cicconi traveled to Italy to visit his sister who had recently recovered from a long illness, she enthusiastically informed him that her doctor had prescribed fresh Mozzarella for her health. Dutifully heeding this advice, she had been eating large quantities of this soft, bland cheese every day. She had become an energetic devotee of Mozzarella. Virgil, swept away by her enthusiasm, also began to partake of it to ensure his own good health. He, too, became convinced of its healing properties, but knew that fresh Mozzarella, as he found it in Italy, was not to be had back home in Los Angeles. He feared he would have to discontinue his new regime. His sister's suggestion that he make it himself caught his fancy. After all, why not? So, he returned to Los Angeles with an idea and the beginnings of a plan to retire from his faltering fishing business and become a cheese maker.

In recent years, Virgil's livelihood as a fisherman had become increasingly precarious and unprofitable. He was catching fewer swordfish but the costs of operating a fishing business were rising. Though fishing was once a lucrative occupation, it no longer made sense to Virgil to take his boat out onto the ocean. At the age of fifty-four, when most people start to think of slowing down, Virgil decided to make a major shift in his career. He would trade swordfish for Mozzarella. The transition was not easy since he knew nothing about making cheese. However, he did have a Sicilian friend with some scant knowledge of the craft. They decided to work together. Learning was a long process of experimentation but, being a proud and stubborn man, Virgil was not one to give up while venturing into an unknown world.

After much time and innumerable attempts and failures, they finally made a curd that would stretch. This is essential for the making of Mozzarella. Having eventually mastered the technique, Virgil was ready to expand their tiny business. He wanted to move from their cramped and inadequate quarters to a larger space and make more cheese in a more controlled environment. Since his friend was quite content to stay where he was, they agreed upon a separation. Virgil found a spot in an industrial park in Torrance, California, and purchased various pieces of new and used equipment.

Virgil knew he needed a better understanding of cheese making. He asked his sister in Italy to find an Italian technician who could help him with his "ferment," the microbial basis for a cheese culture. She found an expert who was willing to travel from Italy to California to help Virgil solve his remaining problems. This man, working in conjunction with his laboratory in Italy, developed a special ferment for Virgil, one that he now uses to make his culture for Italcheese.

Virgil's fascination with things mechanical serves him well. His active imagination guides him in making useful tools of his own design and in adapting used equipment to suit his needs. The tiny processing room we visited was proof of his ingenuity.

In this bright, spotless room Virgil and his son, Marcos, make their cheeses. Their mutual respect and support was quite apparent, as was an underlying sense that they are carefully building something together. While Marcos made that day's Ricotta, they frequently consulted each other. The cheese making here is meticulous, careful, and simple. Their fresh, clean, and bright cheeses are handmade and results are exquisite. The Ricotta is light and fluffy; the Mozzarella is springy but yields when cut. Perhaps their most popular item is their irresistible Bocconcini, tiny balls of Mozzarella, each approximately one inch in diameter.

At the time of our visit, Mascarpone was the latest addition to the roster of their products. This is an Italian version of a thick, buttery cultured cream cheese with a pleasant, slightly acidic tang. Italcheese is one of the few producers of it in America.

After only six months in business, they were processing 425 gallons of milk three times every two weeks. It was evident that the growing popularity of the Italcheese products would soon require an increase in production. Within two years, Virgil had found some investors and moved to a much larger plant in Gardena where, at last count, he was producing eleven products, mostly variously shaped and named versions of his basic Mozzarella. By mid-1988 he was processing 3,500 gallons of milk each week from a dairy in Corona. Though the scale is larger, the players remain the same. Marcos still works with his father, as does Virgil's wife, who is responsible for the bookkeeping.

As is usual in a business so young and so small, Virgil wears many hats. Besides his active involvement in production and personnel management, he handles all of the marketing and sales, calling on his regular accounts for orders and coordinating the manufacture and delivery of the cheese. He does not advertise but relies on word-of-mouth to attract

Italcheese, Inc.

new customers. His principal market is Los Angeles, though he also sends cheese to San Francisco, Miami, and Texas. He is confident that he has the capacity to produce a thousand pounds of Mozzarella a day and is well on his way to achieving that goal.

We sensed an undertone of energy and excitement at Italcheese. Could it be Virgil's feeling that he is at the beginning of something wonderful and that much progress lies ahead for him? Perhaps Virgil expressed it best at the outset of his venture, "I'm poor, but I can do whatever I want. I'm the owner here. I'm even the boss!" When asked three years later how his role had changed in his expanded business, he quipped, "Nothing's changed. I'm just doing more and working longer and harder."

There does appear to be a bright future for Italcheese. Virgil believes the regular consumption of Mozzarella to be the wave of the future and the cure for an ailing society. He believes that, eventually, people will acknowledge and embrace the virtues of this fresh cheese and make it a part of their regular diet. He would like to see Mozzarella as a regular item on hospital menus. Somehow, it seems reasonable that Virgil's medicine, Mozzarella, be served in hospitals. Once the sick are well, they might choose to continue to eat Mozzarella daily, as Virgil does. If his energy and enthusiasm are derived in any way from the ingestion of his cheese, it appears we all might benefit from a daily dose.

Italcheese, Inc.

Odd as it may seem, we think a Mexican accent is appropriate to these Bocconcini. After all, Italcheese is produced in Southern California where Mexican-flavored foods abound. Besides that, the flavors combine beautifully!

2 large garlic cloves, minced
⅔ cup coarsely chopped cilantro
⅔ cup chopped red onion
1 teaspoon ground cumin
½ teaspoon fresh oregano
⅔ cup olive oil
½ cup fresh lime juice
Salt and pepper to taste
6 Bocconcini (approximately ½ pound total), each cut into quarters
1 large or 2 small *poblano* chiles, roasted, skinned, cut into long strips, then cut into thirds
1 Hass avocado, peeled, seeded, and cut into 16 pieces
⅔ cup jicama, peeled, thinly sliced, and cut into matchsticks

Mix the garlic, cilantro, onion, cumin, oregano, oil, lime juice, salt, and pepper. Add the Bocconcini, chiles, avocado, and jicama. Toss lightly and marinate for 15 minutes before serving at room temperature.

South-of-the-Border Bocconcini

Serves 4

Italcheese, Inc.

Grilled Smoked Mozzarella and Prosciutto Dolmas

Serves 4

If fresh grape leaves are available, choose the youngest and most tender of the large-sized leaves. Blanch until soft, usually one to two minutes in simmering water. Drain on paper towels. Use bottled grape leaves if you have no access to fresh ones.

12 garlic cloves, peeled
About 5 tablespoons olive oil
12 grape leaves, blanched
¼ pound prosciutto, thinly sliced
½ pound smoked Mozzarella, cut into ¼-by-½-by-1½-inch slices
1 tablespoon balsamic vinegar
Salt and pepper to taste
Garlic Toasts (recipe follows)

Sauté the peeled garlic in 1 to 2 tablespoons of the olive oil until they are toasty and crunchy. Drain on paper towels.

Flatten each grape leaf and cover it with 1 slice of prosciutto. In the center of the leaf place 1 slice of Mozzarella. Add 1 garlic clove, sliced. Wrap the leaf into a neat package and secure with a toothpick. Brush it with olive oil. Repeat the filling and wrapping with each leaf.

Place the *dolmas* on a hot barbecue grill and lightly brown for approximately 2 minutes on each side. Mix 2 tablespoons olive oil with the vinegar, salt, and pepper to make a vinaigrette to drizzle over the packages. Serve hot off the grill, with Garlic Toasts.

Garlic Toasts
Half a loaf French bread, cut into ¼- to ½-inch slices
Olive oil
1 or 2 large garlic cloves

Brush the bread slices lightly with olive oil. Place on a grill and toast lightly on both sides. Remove from the grill, rub with garlic cloves, and serve.

Italcheese, Inc.

204

The little warmed cheeses here so resemble poached eggs. This unusual first course will elicit surprise and delight.

    2 handfuls young, tender arugula
    2 handfuls young, tender salad greens
    2 tablespoons raspberry vinegar
    6 tablespoons olive oil
    1/2 teaspoon anchovy paste
    3/4 teaspoon Dijon mustard
    4 Bocconcini (approximately 1/3 pound), each cut in half
    Freshly ground black pepper

Wash, dry, and arrange the greens on one large serving plate or on individual plates. Mix the vinegar, oil, anchovy paste, and mustard in a small skillet and heat gently, on the lowest setting. When the mixture is warm, add the Bocconcini halves. Continue heating the mixture until the cheeses are just warmed through. Arrange the warm cheeses on the greens, drizzle with the dressing, and grind some black pepper over the top. Serve immediately.

Devour this tart with a fresh fruit salad for brunch or with sliced, fresh, ripe tomatoes and anchovies for lunch.

Crust
Line a 10-inch tart pan with your favorite savory pastry crust. Bake, with weights, in 400°F oven for 8 to 10 minutes. Leave the oven on.

    Filling
    2 cups basil leaves, finely chopped
    2 tablespoons olive oil
    1 ounce Dry Jack, grated (1/4 cup)
    3 eggs
    1 1/2 pounds Ricotta (3 cups)
    1 teaspoon salt
    1 small head garlic, roasted, cloves peeled
    1/3 cup oil-packed, dried tomatoes, chopped

Mix together all the ingredients and pour into the baked pastry crust. Bake at 400°F for 10 minutes. Lower the heat to 350°F and bake for an additional 20 to 25 minutes. The tart should be firm and lightly browned. Serve warm.

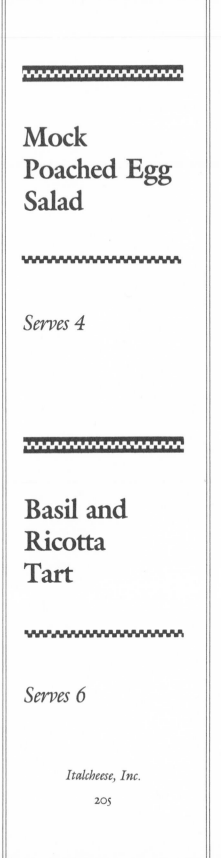

Mock Poached Egg Salad

Serves 4

Basil and Ricotta Tart

Serves 6

Italcheese, Inc.

Fig and Mascarpone Pasta

Serves 4

We have never forgotten eating a dish similar to this one. Memories of it lurked in our minds for years and finally materialized in our version of the ultimate comfort food.

8 ounces dried, or 12 ounces fresh, linguine
2 tablespoons olive oil
½ cup chopped onion
¼ teaspoon turmeric
¼ teaspoon cayenne pepper
¼ teaspoon black mustard seed
8 to 10 large fresh figs or 6 to 8 ounces chopped dried figs
¾ cup heavy cream
4 ounces Mascarpone (½ cup)
Grated Parmesan or Dry Jack (optional)

Cook the linguine al dente.

Meanwhile, heat the olive oil in a skillet and sauté the onion until soft. Stir in the turmeric, cayenne, and mustard seed. Sauté until fragrant. Add the figs and cream. Simmer for 3 minutes if using fresh figs, 5 to 8 minutes if using dried.

Drain the pasta and place in a serving dish. Combine the Mascarpone with the fig mixture, stirring until the cheese is heated. Toss the fig sauce with the pasta and serve hot. Offer the grated cheese.

Italcheese, Inc.

Bulk Farms

....

Escalon
California

Bulk Farms

••••••••••••••••••••

*Escalon
California*

CHEESES: Gouda, Cumin
or Garlic Gouda; Edam
(longer-aged wheels by
order)
RETAIL SALES: By ap-
pointment
TOURS: By appointment
MAIL ORDER: Yes

Just south of the Sacramento River Delta is an area of California not unlike the Netherlands with canals, dams, levees,
and flat farmland. Perhaps this resemblance lured the Bulk
family to settle near the small community of Escalon. Walter
Bulk, the younger son of a Dutch crop farmer, very much
wanted to follow the family tradition of farming. So did his
brother. In Holland the quantity of farm land is finite so the
second son of a small farmer has to look elsewhere for work.
The enterprising Walter Bulk looked to America.

He settled in a fertile California valley carpeted with walnut and almond orchards, vineyards, and dairies. Occasionally, a Dutch name appears on a dairy, store, or produce
stand, suggesting the presence of a community of Dutch de-
scent. Walter married a Dutch woman, Lenneke, who shared
his dream of a life that would have been impossible in their
homeland. Like generations of immigrants before them, they
translated a bit of their native culture into the American way.
The taste of Holland they chose to share is the world-famous
Gouda cheese.

Neither Lenneke nor Walter had made cheese before.
However, Lenneke's sister and Walter's family on his mother's side were cheese makers, so they returned to Holland for
a few weeks to undertake an intensive apprenticeship. They
purchased all of their equipment and cultures and returned to
Escalon to begin the new adventure.

In 1983 they rented a neighbor's barn and converted it to
a cheese-making facility. They were pleased with the cheese
they produced but had difficulty selling it. They chose a distributor who sold their cheese to large supermarket chains
where it was placed beside the imported Gouda and offered
for the same price. This policy was disastrous. As Lenneke
said, "When average consumers are faced with the choice of
an imported product with which they are familiar, and a domestic newcomer for the same price, they will choose the imported." The Bulks knew farming and they knew Gouda, but
were unfamiliar with the distribution game and did not want
to play it. Walter and Lenneke looked for another way to sell
what they knew to be a good product.

The 1980s engendered a phenomenal revival of farmers'
markets. Communities everywhere were providing space for
local farmers to sell their fresh products directly to the consumer. The Bulks decided to sell their cheese at the farmers'
market in nearby Stockton. Easier said than done! Manufac-

tured products were not allowed and, technically, the Bulk cheese, though a handmade, farmstead product, was considered to have been manufactured. Walter was tenacious, applying to the Board of Directors and then applying again. The Board finally gave their approval, which opened the door to farmers' markets in neighboring communities.

The Bulks buy their milk from a local farmer, pasteurize it, then add culture and rennet. After half an hour, the curd is cut into pea-sized pieces with handheld wire cutters. A third of the whey is drained and hot water is added. The curd is stirred for about half an hour and then once again a third of the whey is drained and hot water is added. When the curd reaches the desired consistency, it is gathered into one large 600-pound block, which is cut into sixty squares and transferred to round molds. Walter turns these molds over several times, then leaves them overnight.

The next morning, the cheese is removed from the molds and placed in a salt-water brine for two-and-a-half days. Once out of the brine, the cheese is coated daily for four days with a Dutch plastic and wax substance. This special coating allows the cheese to continue to age, while maintaining its soft texture and protecting it from the growth of mold. After the fourth day, most of the cheeses are wrapped in plastic and left to age. A small percentage of their production, sold primarily to their Dutch neighbors, is left unwrapped so that the traditional dry skin may form while the cheese is aging.

The plain Gouda, immensely popular with all their customers, is their mainstay. They also produce a traditional cumin-flavored Gouda and, in response to consumer demand, a Garlic Gouda. All of their cheeses are flavorful, versatile, and melt well. We found the Cumin Gouda to be extraordinarily tasty in Mexican dishes. Dutch and Mexican cultures, neighbors in California, are uncannily linked by this cheese.

The Bulks maintain a hard and long schedule. For two days a week they make cheese and for another four they travel to sell at various farmers' markets. Planning to expand their market sales and their mail-order business, they will employ a young helper from Holland. Walter enjoys making the cheese and expects to continue that facet of his work as the business grows.

We have been pleasantly surprised when visiting cheese makers in America, to find pockets in which the melting-pot effect has not completely consumed cultural differences. The

Bulks make a cheese much like the one of their homeland. They ride the short distance to the factory on a bicycle, raise their children in the language and traditions of Holland, and share a strong sense of community with others of the same heritage. At the same time they feel pride and affection for their adopted country and are grateful to be here doing what they want. They know that this opportunity would not have been available to them had they stayed home.

A California-style combination of typical Dutch ingredients, this refreshing salad has crunch, color, and flavor. One of the advantages of this salad is that the ingredients are available year-round.

¼ cup lemon juice
¼ cup olive oil
¼ cup safflower oil
1 teaspoon Dijon mustard
Salt and pepper to taste
3 medium white potatoes, cooked, peeled, and cut into matchsticks
1 apple, peeled and cut into matchsticks
1 can sardines or kippered snacks, cut into 1-inch pieces
½ pound Gouda, cut into matchsticks
2 stalks celery, thinly sliced
½ cup chopped Italian parsley leaves
4 small beets, cooked, peeled, and cut into matchsticks

Prepare a vinaigrette with the lemon juice, oils, mustard, salt, and pepper. Mix the potatoes, apple, sardines, Gouda, celery, and parsley together with ¾ of the vinaigrette. Mix the beets with the remaining vinaigrette in a separate bowl. Place the main ingredients in the center of a serving platter. Arrange the beets in a circle around the other ingredients. This salad is best when served at room temperature.

Escalon Salad

Serves 4 to 6

Bulk Farms

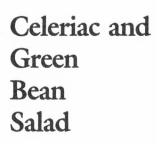

Celeriac and Green Bean Salad

Serves 4

Once fairly rare, celeriac, or celery root, is finally a regular item in the produce section of most supermarkets. In this recipe its nutty flavor complements the walnuts, oil, sherry vinegar, and cheese.

⅓ cup walnut oil
1 tablespoon sherry vinegar
Salt and pepper to taste
1 cup raw celeriac (celery root), julienned
1½ cups green beans, cut into 1-inch pieces and steamed al dente
1 cup walnut pieces, toasted for 5 minutes in a 350°F oven
⅛ cup chopped cilantro leaves
¼ cup chopped red onion
2 ounces sharp Cheddar, julienned
2 ounces Gouda, julienned

Whisk together the oil, vinegar, salt, and pepper to make a dressing. Toss the celeriac, beans, walnuts, cilantro, onion, and both cheeses with the dressing and serve at room temperature.

Assuage your lunch-time hunger with a large wedge of Dutch Potato Tart accompanied by a tossed green salad. Smaller wedges paired with sunny-side-up eggs will enliven a brunch. Or, indulge in a wedge served with a luscious roast chicken or pork for dinner.

¾ pound Gouda, grated (3 cups)
5 large russet potatoes, very thinly sliced but not peeled
Freshly ground black pepper
2 medium onions, peeled and thinly sliced
¼ pound Black Forest ham, very thinly sliced
3 to 5 tablespoons butter

Preheat the oven to 425° F.

Butter a round baking dish that measures 10 inches in diameter and 1½ inches high.

Arrange a third of the potato slices, overlapped, to cover the bottom. Lightly pepper the potatoes. Layer with half of the onion, then half of the ham, and then, a third of the cheese. Repeat the layers of potato, pepper, onion, ham, and cheese. Finish with a layer of potato and a generous grinding of black pepper. Dot with 3 tablespoons of the butter.

Bake in the preheated oven for 40 minutes. Remove and sprinkle with the reserved cup of cheese. Return to the oven for 10 minutes. Serve hot or warm.

Dutch Potato Tart

Serves 6

Bulk Farms

Gouda Quesadillas with Pineapple Salsa

Serves 4

If you are short on time, use prepared tortillas in place of the homemade ones. The unusual salsa is a knock-out!

1½ cups *masa harina* (white corn meal)
½ teaspoon salt
1 egg
¾ cup plus 1 tablespoon water
6 ounces Cumin Gouda, cut into 8 equal pieces
Cooking oil

Mix the *masa harina*, salt, egg, and ¾ cup water until a smooth ball forms. Divide into 8 equal balls. Roll out each ball between waxed paper to a thickness of approximately ¹/₁₆ inch or as thin as you can without breaking the tortilla shape.

Place a piece of cheese in the middle, fold the dough in half, trim, and seal the edges with water. Pinch the seam decoratively or score with fork tines.

Pour oil into a heavy skillet until it is approximately ½ inch deep. Heat until hot but not smoking. Carefully lower the *quesadillas* into the hot oil. Fry until golden brown. Flip and repeat on the other side. The total frying time is 3 to 5 minutes. Drain on paper towels. Serve hot with Pineapple Salsa (recipe follows).

Pineapple Salsa
2 cups fresh pineapple, diced
2 to 4 garlic cloves, minced
1 or 2 *jalapeño* peppers, minced
¼ cup coarsely chopped cilantro leaves
Salt to taste

Mix all the ingredients and set aside for 30 minutes for the flavors to blend. Serve at room temperature.

Ferrante, Father and Son

Forming Mozzarella balls

Ferrante Cheese Company

▭▭▭▭▭▭▭▭▭▭▭▭

*Martinez
California*

CHEESES: Mozzarella,
  Bocconcini, Ricotta
RETAIL SALES: Yes
TOURS: No
MAIL ORDER: No

Mozzarella Fresca

▭▭▭▭▭▭▭▭▭▭▭▭

*Benicia
California*

CHEESES: Mozzarella,
  Bocconici, Ricotta
RETAIL SALES: Yes
TOURS: No
MAIL ORDER: No

What impoverished lives we would lead were it not for the Italians! Consider for a moment some of their contributions: Florence and Venice, Michelangelo and Da Vinci, Vivaldi, and Verdi, and of course, Italian shoes. Food lovers all over the world delight in the legacy of scrumptious creations such as pasta, dried tomatoes, prosciutto, and innumerable flavors, shapes, and styles of cheese. Luckily for us, Italian emigrants have often aimed their sights at the fair shores of these United States. Large communities of Italian-Americans abound in our major cities, and it is usually only in these communities that one can obtain sweet, fresh Mozzarella and Ricotta. In small shops in New York and Boston, curd is hand-worked into fist-sized Mozzarella or small, egg-shaped Bocconicini. It is the privilege of the city dweller to slip into one of these shops any day and saunter out the proud possessor of a little fresh Ricotta or a newly made Mozzarella.

However, most of us are proffered only the processed, vacuum-wrapped, rubberized supermarket versions of these cheeses. Even San Francisco, with its large Italian community, cannot claim a neighborhood Mozzarella factory. But, across San Francisco Bay, in the unlikely setting of a suburban shopping center, there was a glowing light. When we heard of the Ferrante Cheese Company we rushed to see just how heaven on earth had landed in such a curious location.

Roberto Ferrante was brining and wrapping one-pound Mozzarella balls when we arrived. One by one, he removed the balls from a salt brine, dropped each into a plastic bag, then heat-sealed the bags. He continued his work as he revealed to us the story of his family's odyssey from Italy to their cheese business in California.

Roberto's father, Vincenzo Ferrante, grew up in the dairy region that surrounds Palermo in Italy. He spent his childhood in the mountains visiting farmers and cheese makers. Vincenzo, unlike others of his age, was not interested in games. He spent his days with local cheese makers, pestering them until they put him to work. He began his career at the ripe old age of twelve and, through the years, he learned to make many Italian cheeses. Eventually, disillusioned with his homeland and lured by the dream of America, he, like many before him, emigrated to New York. In 1962, Vincenzo's wife and six children followed him to America.

For almost twenty years, Vincenzo worked in cheese factories in New York and Florida. He always harbored the desire to work for himself but needed the help of his sons to begin such an ambitious endeavor. However, as with most families, the children grew up and had their own interests. The eldest, Miguele, disappeared for a few years, showing up at San Francisco's Fisherman's Wharf with 25 cents in his pocket. The youngest, Roberto, a basketball player in college, eventually returned to Italy as a professional athlete. The daughters married and other sons, too, went their own ways.

With characteristic warmth, the Italian community of San Francisco helped Miguele with a little money and a job. By the late 1970s he had parlayed that help into the ownership of a restaurant in Moraga, California. With one son well established in the Bay Area, the Ferrante family began to visit. They were all entranced with the mountains, the trees, and the Pacific. It all looked "real good" to them, coming from Brooklyn, so, one by one the children moved to California. With almost all of their children in the San Francisco area, Vincenzo and his wife retired and joined them there.

At about this time, Roberto decided to give up the life of a professional basketball player in Italy. He, too, was drawn to the California life but knew he would need to find a new way to support himself there. Luckily, Vincenzo had a dim view of retirement. Unwilling to be idle, he had been making sausage and cheese in small quantities for his son's restaurant. Vincenzo and Roberto became a team. "Let's try making a little more and see if we can sell it." Roberto described it thusly, "You want California? You better make cheese!" Finding a location in which they could manufacture their cheese was their first hurdle. Vincenzo and his wife do not drive, therefore production facilities had to be within walking distance to their home. They considered it auspicious when one of Roberto's sisters found a small storefront in a shopping center approximately one block from the Ferrante home. Cautiously, slowly, they increased their production.

The day of our visit, the phone was ringing off the hook. Restaurants all over the Bay Area order Ferrante cheese and their client list reads like a guide to fine dining: Chez Panisse, Square One, Café Fanny, and Prego, to name a few. At the time, every week they produced approximately nine hundred pounds each of Mozzarella and Ricotta in their small facility. Vincenzo, Roberto, and another brother were the only employees in this new family business. The opportunity to grow was there if they chose to take it and, before long, Roberto made that choice and opened his own business, Mozzarella Fresca, in Benicia. The result of his decision is that there are now two cheese businesses owned and operated by two generations of Ferrantes. The following account of the cheese-making process is as it was when we visited them both in the shopping center, and still is for Vincenzo in his new Martinez plant.

Vincenzo's process is extremely labor-intensive. Fresh milk is pasteurized and a buttermilk starter is added to the vat. Rennet is added and, after twenty to twenty-five minutes, paddles are used to break up the curd. The whey that rises to the top is pumped into another tank. The curd is then scooped onto a draining table and cut, to allow the whey to drain better. The curds are left to ripen for several hours. In the evening, Vincenzo returns to check his curd for elasticity. If it is just right, he refrigerates the curd until the next morning. After working with his father for some time, Roberto has grasped the "feel." However, he remarks, with some humility, "The milk, the weather, anything can affect the cheese. If you don't really understand, it can blow your mind. Maybe you did the same thing yesterday, but today it is completely different."

The following morning, the Mozzarella curd is pressed through a slicing device into a tub, hot water is added, and the mass is stirred until it reaches a consistent texture. At this moment, once again, the cheese maker's discretion comes into play. In Vincenzo's words, "You must understand the cheese." When the texture is right, the balls are formed by hand, dropped into cold water, lightly brined, and then packaged. This cheese is best eaten as fresh as possible, preferably within a week and a half, or at most 3 weeks if packed in Cryovac plastic wrap. The life of the cheese may be extended by freezing.

The Ricotta process is relatively simple. The whey reserved from the Mozzarella curd is heated to 160 degrees. Some milk is added and the mixture is heated further to 184 degrees. The addition of vinegar curdles the solids and sends them rising to the surface. A sweet, lactic fragrance emanates as the curds cook. The Ricotta is ladled into perforated plastic molds and allowed to drain. That is all there is to it. The manufacture of Ricotta makes use of most of the whey, eliminates waste, and simultaneously engenders some profit.

At Roberto's facility in Benicia, a more automated technique is used. Modern equipment replaces much of the hand labor and increases his production capacity. His wife, Joanne, designed their label and acts, among other things, as pasteurizer of their milk. Roberto, the gentle giant, has made cheese making his sport, bringing to it the same passion and commitment that he once felt for basketball. These two young Ferrantes, ambitious and energetic, are taking all the steps necessary to expand their business to fit their vision. That vision includes large volume, new cheeses, and even franchising.

Roberto knows that he is fortunate to have had the rare experience of working with his father. Concerned for the future of his growing family and fired by the ambition and energy of youth, he needed to expand. Vincenzo, on the other hand, is content to continue in his own style at his own pace. Perhaps their success will encourage others to enter the world of cheese manufacturing, hard work though it may be, so that one day we all might find a store-front Mozzarella factory in our neighborhood shopping center.

Ricotta Pancakes

These versatile pancakes can grace any meal, at any time of day. Serve them at breakfast, brunch, as an accompaniment to a main dinner course, or as a midnight snack. If a sweet pancake is desired, use the basic recipe and serve the pancakes with a sprinkling of powdered sugar, fresh fruit, or maple syrup. Savory pancakes may be served plain or with grated Parmesan cheese. The recipes given below are for three variations of pancake and two accompanying sauces.

Serves 6
Approximately 20 pancakes 3 inches in diameter

Basic Pancakes
6 eggs, separated and at room temperature
1 pound Ricotta (2 cups)
1 tablespoon sugar
1 teaspoon salt
¾ cup all-purpose flour

Beat the egg yolks in a large bowl. Add the Ricotta, beating until well mixed. Blend in the sugar, salt, and flour, being careful not to overmix.

Beat the egg whites until stiff and then gently fold them into the Ricotta mixture.

Pour approximately half a cup of the mixture onto a greased hot griddle. When lightly browned, flip the pancake and cook on the other side until browned.

Wild Rice Pancake
1 recipe basic Ricotta Pancakes
3 cups cooked wild rice

Combine the wild rice with the basic pancake mixture. Follow the cooking directions given for basic pancakes. Serve with Pear Coulis (recipe follows).

Fontina Tortilla
4 ounces Fontina, grated (1 cup)
1½ teaspoons hot red chile, seeded and chopped
1½ cups corn kernels, fresh or frozen
1 recipe basic Ricotta Pancakes

Combine Fontina, chiles, and corn with the basic pancake mixture. Follow the cooking directions given for basic pancakes. Serve with Tomato and Cilantro Sauce (recipe follows).

Ferrante, Father and Son

Blue Cheese Pancakes

3 ounces Blue Cheese, crumbled
1½ cups walnuts or pecans, chopped
1 recipe basic Ricotta Pancakes

Combine the Blue Cheese and nuts with the basic pancake mixture. Follow the cooking directions given for basic pancakes. Serve with Pear Coulis (recipe follows).

Pear Coulis
Makes approximately 3 cups.

6 pears, peeled, cored, and chopped
1 cup sugar
2 teaspoons grated lemon zest
2 teaspoons grated fresh ginger
½ teaspoon mace

Combine the pears with the sugar, lemon zest, ginger, and mace. Cook over low heat in a sauté pan until the mixture resembles coarse applesauce. Serve warm with pancakes.

Tomato and Cilantro Sauce
Makes approximately 1½ cups.

8 Roma tomatoes, peeled, seeded, and finely chopped
2 tablespoons light soy, peanut, or corn oil
½ cup chopped fresh cilantro leaves
Salt and freshly ground pepper, to taste

Combine all the ingredients. Serve at room temperature.

Ricotta Custard with Blueberry Sauce

Serves 6

We celebrate the short blueberry season with this dessert, a showcase for both blueberries and fresh Ricotta.

Custard
¾ pound Ricotta (1½ cups)
½ cup heavy cream
1 teaspoon vanilla extract
2 eggs
2 egg yolks
⅛ cup sugar
Butter
1 cup heavy cream, whipped (optional)

Preheat the oven to 325°F.

In a food processor or a medium mixing bowl, mix the Ricotta, the ½ cup cream, vanilla, eggs and egg yolks, and sugar until well blended.

Fill 6 buttered ½-cup soufflé dishes or custard cups with the cheese mixture. Set the molds in a baking pan and pour boiling water into the pan until it reaches halfway up the sides of the cups. Bake in the preheated oven for 35 minutes or until a toothpick inserted in the custard comes out clean. Remove from the oven and allow to cool for 10 minutes. Run a knife around the outside edges of the custards.

Spoon an equal amount of blueberry sauce on each of 6 serving plates. Invert the custards onto the sauce. Top with whipped cream, if desired. Decorate with the reserved blueberries.

Blueberry Sauce
2 cups fresh blueberries
¼ cup sugar
¼ cup water
¼ teaspoon allspice
1 tablespoon lemon juice

Reserve 18 berries for decorating the custard. In a small saucepan, combine the remaining berries, sugar, water, allspice, and lemon juice. Simmer for approximately 5 minutes, until the sauce thickens and the blueberries soften. Remove from heat and set aside.

Ferrante, Father and Son

In this warm salad, the heat from the sautéed oysters softens the Mozzarella and highlights its subtle flavor. Teamed with the spicy oriental dressing, the combination is irresistible.

Juice of 1 lime
1½-inch piece of fresh ginger, grated or chopped
1 large garlic clove
1 teaspoon Szechwan pepper
1 teaspoon soy sauce
1 teaspoon sesame oil
¼ cup peanut or soy oil
½ pound fresh Mozzarella, cut in 1-inch cubes
10 ounces fresh oysters
½ cup all-purpose flour, seasoned with salt and pepper
¼ cup vegetable oil
1 bunch leaf lettuce, red or green

In a blender or food processor, mix the lime juice, ginger, garlic, Szechwan pepper, soy sauce, sesame oil, and peanut oil until smooth. Place the Mozzarella cubes in a small bowl and pour over them the lime juice mixture. Set aside.

Drain the oysters and then dry them with paper towels. If they are large, cut in halves or quarters. Dredge the oysters in seasoned flour. Heat the vegetable oil in a skillet. Fry the oysters for 2 minutes on each side.

Arrange the lettuce on a serving platter. Remove the cheese from the lime juice mixture with a slotted spoon and arrange in a circle on the greens. Place the hot oysters on the cheese. Drizzle with the remaining dressing.

Oyster Salad with Ginger Vinaigrette

Serves 4

Ferrante, Father and Son

Sonoma
Cheese
Factory

*Sonoma
California*

Sonoma Cheese Factory

~~~~~~~~~~~~~~~~~~~~~~

Sonoma
California

CHEESES: Jack, Flavored
   Jack, Low-Salt Jack,
   Cheddar
RETAIL SALES: Yes
TOURS: Viewing window
   and video
MAIL ORDER: Yes

Sonoma Cheese factory chronicles three distinct stages typical in the history of America's small-scale cheese producers. Immigrant cheese makers arrived and ambitiously put their old-world skills to work in their new home. Later, the entire industry had to adjust to significant technological changes that made possible increased production and better quality control. In the present world the key is specialization and marketing. Throughout these changes, Sonoma's Viviani family has endured and thrived.

It all began with Celso Viviani, a strong, physically energetic man from the marble-cutting region near Lucca in Italy. He arrived in California in 1912 to work near Sonoma, in the quarries that furnished stones for the streets and buildings of San Francisco. Celso and others new to the area found in northern California a temperate climate, fertile land, and unlimited resources that enabled them to recreate some of the pleasures of their homeland. Since, for the Italians, wine was essential, it was only natural that Celso and his newly arrived brother, Nonnie, would help the legendary Sebastiani family build their winery. They continued working for Sebastiani Winery until Prohibition put a stop to that bit of fun. Another fermentation process lured them to work for Joe and Tom Vella in a local cheese factory. Eventually Celso Viviani and Tom Vella became partners and opened their own plant. Meanwhile, Joe Vella (Tom's brother) and Nonnie Viviani continued to operate the original factory. Thus the community of Sonoma had two cheese plants operated by two sets of brothers—one Viviani and one Vella in each plant.

Through the 1930s the California landscape was dotted with hundreds of small cheese plants. The lack of refrigeration and efficient, speedy transportation meant that milk had to be transformed into cheese virtually as it left the cow. Major changes in mechanization, sanitation, and technology forced the Sonoma cheese plants to change if they were to survive. For example, initially milk was cooled by placing the ten-gallon cans of milk in a cold-water bath, a method still practiced by Amish farmers. Most dairymen today cool their machine-pumped milk in large refrigerated tanks. Five- and ten-gallon cans of milk are no longer hauled in the back of horse-drawn wagons or pick-up trucks; witness today's ubiquitous refrigerated milk trucks coursing our interstate highways.

Among other factors the costs of these changes soon made it unfeasible for many small plants to survive. Most closed, large co-ops were formed, and Kraft and Borden bought or contracted with many of the remaining small local plants. The Viviani-Vella partnerships weathered these changes. By the 1940s, each partnership owned two plants, had contracted with Kraft, and was making Cottage Cheese and dry and condensed milk.

More changes were in store after World War II. The Viviani and Vella partnerships dissolved and the Viviani family retained the present site on the square in Sonoma. (For the further adventures of the Vella family, see the account of Vella's Bear Flag cheese factory, on page 233.) By the 1960s the businesses of both families were suffering. Milk prices and other costs were high; cheese prices were low. By then, Celso's son, Pete, was at the helm. He had grown up in the cheese business and it was proverbially "in his blood." Despite a lifetime in the cheese business, even Pete was discouraged.

New life was breathed into the business when Pete's son, David, joined his father in the family business and focused on the delicatessen store in front of the cheese plant. Soon they were selling sandwiches in schools, at the racetrack, and to local businesses. As the deli business expanded, the Vivianis began to produce their cheese under the label of Sonoma Jack.

The Vivianis' turnaround began in the 1970s when Sonoma, in the heart of a burgeoning wine region, became a mecca for tourists. Visitors began to find in quaint Sonoma a perfect escape from the city hustle, a charming place to taste local wines, enjoy the town square, and picnic on bread and cheese. The Sonoma Cheese Factory is prominent on the north side of the city square and this good fortune spelled the rebirth of the successful Viviani cheese business.

Visitors to the Sonoma plant witness the time-honored tradition of cheese making practiced by the Vivianis. After rennet is added to the milk and the curds are cut, they are gathered into large square cheesecloths and rolled into one-, three-, and eleven-pound wheels. The wheels are stacked and pressed overnight. This process fashions unevenly shaped wheels with creases on the underside, evidence of the tightly twisted cheesecloth wrapping. Once unwrapped, the wheels are turned twice a day for two days and then allowed to mellow for about three days. They are vacuum-wrapped whole, or cut, labeled, boxed, and shipped.

Today the Sonoma Cheese Factory is managed by Pete, who is the vice-president of the company, David, who is the director of marketing and public relations, and Fred Harland, David's brother-in-law, who is the cheese maker and a co-owner. The product line is expanding. The best seller is the plain Jack, a high-moisture cheese with a semisoft texture and a mild flavor. Other products include Jack flavored with garlic, pepper, or caraway, a young, mild Cheddar, and a cheese they call Teleme. In answer to modern dietary demands, they now also make a Jack to which no salt has been added.

From the ambitious kid selling deli sandwiches to schools, David Viviani has grown to be a well-known public relations and marketing expert. He is knowledgeable about all aspects of the dairy industry and about cheese making, having, like his father, grown up in the cheese factory. Now he concentrates his efforts on marketing the growing line of Sonoma Jack products, and is active in numerous dairy and cheese organizations. He is a fountain of statistics, facts, and marketing schemes. David emphasizes the age-old connection between cheese and wine. He served us cubed samples of his cheese in wine glasses, allowing the nose to better discern the aroma of the cheese and reminding the brain of the affinity cheese has with wine. David associates the two even more closely when he touts the value of his naturally made cheese. "Pasteurized processed cheese is like wine with a screw cap. Natural cheese is like wine with a cork."

Another lodestar of David's is the protection of his product's name. When someone dared to make a processed cheese, called it Jack, and tried to sell it in California, David lobbied and successfully passed a bill that, in effect, defined *Jack* and determined how the name could be used.

He feels that a healthy California cheese industry is good for Sonoma Jack, and enjoys participating in the larger picture. He has been instrumental in directing large amounts of California Dairy Board money toward cheese promotions such as the "California Real Cheese" labeling and advertising campaign. David explains, "Californians eat more cheese than other Americans, though most cheese has traditionally been made in the Midwest. Therefore, an increase in California cheese production makes all the sense in the world. After all, you don't sell cheese to cows."

Unquestionably, David Viviani is a crusader. The momentous strides achieved by the Sonoma Cheese Factory in the last decade are largely a result of his relentless marketing and promotion. It was David, more than any other person, who impressed upon us a secret of success for small-production cheese businesses today. Making the highest quality, best-tasting cheese in America is of little value if people do not buy it. One must attract the consumer's attention and then keep him or her happy. To do that, one must be tireless and innovative. Being a high-profile California cheese maker is advantageous, because as David says, "The view only changes for the lead dog."

Michael recommends this delicacy for dessert or as an appetizer. We like it for those odd times when an unusual snack is in order: Superbowl Sunday, as a treat for a late-arriving guest, or as an unconventional delight at tea time.

8 ounces Jack, sliced
5 tablespoons butter
¾ cup brown sugar
1 ounce shredded sweet coconut
2 ounces macadamia nuts, chopped
½ cup dark rum

Arrange the cheese on a shallow heat-resistant serving platter.

In a medium saucepan, melt the butter over medium heat. Just before the butter browns, add the sugar and stir constantly until it dissolves. Add the coconut and nuts, continuing to stir until warmed and well mixed. Remove the saucepan from the heat. Add the rum. Return to the heat and ignite the mixture. Immediately pour it over the cheese.

Serve with unsalted crackers as an appetizer or with apple wedges as a dessert.

▰▰▰▰▰▰▰▰▰▰▰▰▰▰

Michael Clark's Jack Brulée

▰▰▰▰▰▰▰▰▰▰▰▰▰▰

Serves 4

Stuffed Peppers with Summer Squash and Basil

Serves 4

Summer brings a proliferation of peppers, many of which would be suitable in this recipe if you cannot find the sweet and flavorful long Italian ones. Serve these vinaigrette-baked peppers alongside roast or grilled beef or pork.

4 long Italian sweet peppers (*corno di toros*)
¾ cup finely diced fresh, young, summer squash
3 garlic cloves
2 tablespoons plus 1 teaspoon chopped fresh basil
4 ounces Jack, grated (1 cup)
Freshly ground black pepper
2 medium tomatoes, peeled, seeded, and chopped
1 tablespoon red wine vinegar
3 tablespoons olive oil

Place the peppers on a grill or over a flame to char lightly and soften. Cool, then carefully cut through the top side, lengthwise. Remove the seeds.

Steam the squash and 2 of the garlic cloves over boiling water until soft. Cool. Mince the steamed garlic cloves and mix them with the squash, 2 tablespoons basil, and the cheese. Add a generous grinding of black pepper.

Preheat the oven to 400°F. Stuff each pepper with a quarter of the cheese mixture and arrange them in a small baking dish. Mix the tomatoes, vinegar, olive oil, remaining basil, and the third garlic clove in a blender or food processor. Pour this over the peppers and bake in the preheated oven for 10 minutes. Serve immediately.

A contrapuntal spicy cilantro salsa sets off the sweetness of summer corn in this composition. Melted Jack harmonizes with the two. Encore! Encore!

Corn Cakes

2 eggs, separated
2 cups corn kernels, blanched
¼ cup corn flour (available in natural food stores)
¼ cup milk
1 teaspoon baking powder
Salt and pepper, to taste
4 tablespoons butter
2 ounces Jack, cut in four slices

In a medium bowl beat the egg yolks and mix in the corn, corn flour, milk, baking powder, salt, and pepper. Beat the egg whites until stiff. Gently fold the beaten egg whites into the egg and corn mixture.

In a 6-inch omelet pan or skillet, melt 1 tablespoon butter. When hot, ladle in a quarter of the mixture and swirl evenly. When browned, flip. Place 1 slice of cheese on the browned top. Remove from the pan when the underside of the cake has browned. Keep warm.

Repeat with the remaining butter, corn mixture, and cheese until all 4 cakes are cooked. Serve hot with Cilantro Salsa.

Cilantro Salsa

1 bunch cilantro, roots and large stems removed
1 garlic clove, peeled
Half a small *jalapeño* chile
Juice of 1 lime
3 tablespoons peanut or corn oil
½ teaspoon salt
4 Roma tomatoes, peeled, seeded, and coarsely chopped

Purée the cilantro, garlic, chile, lime juice, oil, and salt in a food processor or blender until smooth. Pour into a small bowl. Stir in the tomatoes and set aside.

Corn Cakes with Cilantro Salsa

Makes 4 cakes, each 6 inches in diameter

Sonoma Cheese Factory

Grilled Chicken "Sandwiches" with Caper Sauce

Serves 4

Here, grilled chicken breasts replace bread in ham and cheese sandwiches enlivened by a piquant caper sauce.

2 whole chicken breasts, boned and skinned
1 tablespoon fresh lemon juice
2 tablespoons olive or vegetable oil
¼ teaspoon each salt and pepper
4 ounces Jack, thinly sliced
4 ounces Black Forest ham or prosciutto, thinly sliced
2 tablespoons butter
2 garlic cloves, chopped
2 anchovy fillets, rinsed and chopped
½ cup white wine
1 tablespoon capers
Freshly grated black pepper

Halve the chicken breasts. Lay them flat between two pieces of waxed paper and pound them until the meat is approximately ¼-inch thick. Cut each half breast into two equal pieces.

For the marinade, mix the lemon juice, oil, salt, and pepper. Coat both sides of the chicken pieces with the marinade and let them sit for approximately 30 minutes.

Prepare a hot grill. Divide the cheese and ham and distribute equally onto 4 of the chicken pieces. Cover with the remaining pieces. Secure with toothpicks and set aside.

Melt the butter in skillet over low heat. Sauté the garlic for approximately 2 minutes. Mix in the anchovies, stirring to dissolve them. Pour in the wine. Increase the heat and reduce the mixture by half. Add the capers and a generous grinding of black pepper. Keep this sauce warm.

Grill the chicken for approximately 3 minutes on each side until the meat is cooked through and the cheese melted. Serve hot in a pool of caper sauce or drizzle the sauce on the "sandwiches."

Sonoma Cheese Factory

Coating the cheese with a mixture of oil, cocoa, and pepper

Vella's
Bear Flag

••••••••••••••••••

Sonoma
California

CHEESES: Fresh Jack, Dry
  Jack, Flavored Jacks,
  Cheddar, and Feta
RETAIL SALES: Yes
TOURS: By appointment
MAIL ORDER: Yes

From the early days Sonoma, California, has attracted a size-able community of Italian immigrants whose culinary traditions contributed to the flavor of the town. Since the first decade of the twentieth century, the Vella family has been active in the community, all the while carving a niche for themselves in history. Enterprising Tom Vella, founder of the Vella Cheese Company, has been followed by his equally colorful son, Ignazio, in the stewardship of their family business.

The American chapter of this family history began when Joe Vella, Tom's oldest brother, ventured to the New World in 1906. He opened the Sonoma Mission Creamery, the first cheese factory in Sonoma, and was also part of an enterprise in San Francisco that imported and distributed Italian cheeses. With the advent of World War I, the Italian grating cheeses were no longer easily available, so Joe began producing them in his creamery in Sonoma. In 1923 Tom Vella joined his brother in Sonoma to make cheese.

One day a group of farmers wanting a higher price for their milk asked Tom to open a creamery to compete with the then veritable monopoly, Sonoma Mission Creamery. When they promised him a guaranteed daily quantity of milk, he contracted with them at a higher price than that paid by the Creamery. In partnership with Celso Viviani, one of the cheese makers at the Creamery, he established the Vella Cheese Factory. (For a history of the Viviani family's cheese-making businesses, also in Sonoma, see the account of the Sonoma Cheese Factory on page 225.) In 1931 they leased an old brewery, closed by Prohibition, that houses the Vella Cheese Company today.

In the mid-thirties they contracted to sell their product, Dry Jack, to Kraft. The relationship with Kraft was to be felic-itous: Kraft had a strong research and development team, good knowledge of quality control, and state-of-the-art equipment. World War II, which brought a substantial demand from military bases in the San Francisco area, proved to be a prosperous time for Vella.

Tom and Celso dissolved their partnership in 1948, when some of Celso's five children wanted to play a larger role in the business. Tom retained the factory they had acquired in Oregon and the Vivianis kept the Sonoma facility built by Tom and Celso in the early forties. Three years later, Joe retired and the other stockholders decided to close the Sonoma branch. Tom returned to Sonoma to open his own factory in what was formerly the Sonoma Mission Creamery.

From the time he was seven, Tom's son, Ignazio, had worked in his father's cheese factory, making wooden shipping boxes after school. Through the years, he learned to oil the aging cheeses, wax and box the finished cheeses and, eventually, to take charge of the shipping.

Ignazio went to a military high school and then to Santa Clara University, from which, in 1950, he graduated, *magna cum laude,* with a Bachelor of Science degree in history. Then he spent a year in Italy. In all, he was absent from the daily life of the cheese factory for eight years. When he returned to Sonoma, Tom was putting together his own creamery so Ignazio worked with his father for one and a half years before going to the Korean War. In 1955, he once again returned to Sonoma, his father, and the Creamery, where he remained until 1963.

Tensions between father and son erupted in a momentous argument one day, and Ignazio left. For two years he worked in San Francisco as a butter maker and then as a creamery warehouse supervisor. When his father asked him to return, Ignazio declined, wishing to wait until, he said, "I felt I could come back on my own terms." In 1964, he was elected county supervisor for Sonoma County, a position he retained for eleven years, after which he spent six years as County Fair Manager.

In 1981, Ignazio did return to the Creamery on his own terms: his father had given the business to him and his three sisters. He set about repairing the building and equipment that had not been maintained for years and, when necessary, purchased new equipment. He tripled the cheese storage space in the factory and then increased production accordingly. Today, the Vella Cheese Factory is sparkling clean, neat, and organized.

The biggest seller and most popular cheese is his prize-winning Dry Jack, followed by the flavored varieties (*jalapeño,* garlic, caraway, and onion) of Monterey, the wheel-shaped Jack, and Cheddar, which ranges from mild to sharp. Vella's fresh, wheel Monterey Jack is unlike any other Monterey we have sampled. Soft and rich tasting, it is low in salt (.9 percent) and is not a high-moisture product. Ignazio loves this "real Jack" and waxes poetic about its flavor and texture. It used to be known as "table cheese," always left on the table with a glass cover. It would become unctuous, soft, and runny and was used in place of butter.

The richly flavored Dry Jack is coated with cocoa, pepper, and oil and aged for nine months. It attains a buttery, nutty quality not unlike a Parmesan but less piquant and grainy. It is firm enough in texture to be grated but is also easily sliced. Ignazio produces a cheese of character and consistency. "There is no trick to making cheese. Anybody can make cheese. The trick is to make it good. And then the next trick is to make it consistently good."

Milk for the Vella cheeses comes from nearby Sonoma dairies, delivered when it is less than twenty-four hours old. The Guernsey cows that provide this milk are a breed especially well suited to the low hills surrounding Sonoma. According to Ignazio, "By genealogy these cows do not take well to mud or lowlands, or to high country. They are smart cows."

When Tom Vella granted control of the business to his son, Ignazio could not ignore the gift of his heritage. Even though he grew up in the cheese business, he spent many years away from it, not necessarily expecting to return. Yet, he felt compelled to carry on the enterprise started by his father and recognized an opportunity to make a languid business prosperous. Also, Ignazio wants to preserve flavor and honesty in cheese making; the historian wishing to preserve tradition. But more fundamentally, this business is instinctual. He has that feel that is necessary in cheese making. His hands know what to do. He is proud of his meticulously maintained equipment and of his old brick building. His reward is tangible: he can see the effects of his work; he can see history in the making and his role in it. He has kept alive a legacy begun by his dynamic father and has carefully provided a future for his children, an opportunity for them to carry on the tradition.

Michael Clark shared one of his favorite creations with us. What is cleverly disguised as a simple roasted lamb, reveals, when sliced, a filling as delightful to the eye as it is to the tongue.

1 leg of lamb, boned and butterflied
½ pound Jack, cut into thin strips
½ cup chopped walnuts
3 ounces chopped fresh basil
2 garlic cloves, chopped
Salt and freshly ground pepper

Preheat the oven to 375°F.

Pound the butterflied lamb leg to flatten it. Layer the cheese slices on the lamb. Sprinkle the nuts, basil, and garlic evenly over the cheese. Season generously with salt and pepper. Carefully roll up the lamb and tie it tightly.

Place on a rack in a roasting pan. Roast in the preheated oven for 15 minutes per pound. Allow to rest for 15 to 20 minutes after removing from the oven. Remove the string and slice so that each portion contains some filling.

Stuffed Leg of Lamb

Serves 6

Vella's Bear Flag

Spinach and Corned Beef Fusilli

Serves 6 to 8

This is a rich and zesty twist to the traditional noodle casserole.

2 bunches fresh spinach, washed, stems removed, and coarsely chopped, or 2 boxes chopped, frozen spinach
4 eggs, beaten
1 cup sour cream
2 cups milk
1 pound Jack, grated (4 cups)
4 ounces Dry Jack, grated (1 cup)
1 tablespoon Dijon mustard
1 teaspoon salt
½ teaspoon freshly ground black pepper
1 pound fusilli (corkscrew) noodles
½ pound cooked corned beef, cut into bite-sized pieces

Steam fresh spinach until just wilted. Drain thoroughly. If using frozen spinach, thaw and drain, squeezing out as much moisture as possible.

In a large bowl, mix the eggs, sour cream, milk, cheeses, mustard, salt, and pepper. Cook the fusilli al dente. Preheat the oven to 400°F.

Drain the fusilli thoroughly and stir into the egg mixture. Mix in the spinach and corned beef. Pour into a 9-by-13-inch buttered baking dish. Bake in the preheated oven for 20 to 30 minutes, or until set.

There are almost as many stories about the origin of Caesar Salad as there are recipes for it. Here is our version. Maybe Ignazio Vella, the historian, has a story.

    4 slices French bread
    4 garlic cloves, pressed
    ¾ cup olive oil
    1½ teaspoons anchovy paste or 2 anchovy fillets
    1 teaspoon Dijon mustard
    1 egg yolk
    Juice of half a lemon
    Dash of Worcestershire sauce
    Dash of Tabasco sauce
    1 head romaine lettuce, washed, dried, and leaves torn
    3 ounces Dry Jack, coarsely grated (¾ cup)
    Generous amount of freshly ground black pepper

Preheat the oven to 350°F.

Rub the bread slices with one quarter of the garlic and brush generously with olive oil. Cut into 1-inch cubes and toast in the preheated oven until lightly browned.

In a large wooden salad bowl, mix the remaining garlic, the anchovy and the mustard. Add the egg yolk, lemon juice, Worcestershire sauce, and Tabasco. Mix thoroughly. Mix in the ¾ cup olive oil. Add the romaine leaves, tossing to coat. Add the toasted bread cubes, cheese, and freshly ground black pepper. Toss until well mixed. Serve immediately.

Caesar Salad

Serves 4

Vella's Bear Flag

Fried Jack with Garlic Sauce

Serves 4

This lively first course should please any dedicated garlic lover.

2 ounces Jack, sliced ¼-inch thick
1 cup all-purpose flour
3 eggs
1 cup bread crumbs, preferably sourdough
2 large garlic cloves, peeled and blanched
3 tablespoons olive oil
1 teaspoon white wine vinegar
½ cup peanut oil
2 tablespoons minced parsley

Beat 2 of the eggs together in a small bowl. Dredge the cheese first in the flour, then in egg, and then in the bread crumbs. Refrigerate for at least 20 minutes.

In a blender or food processor, mix the garlic, the remaining egg, olive oil, and vinegar until frothy and thickened. Set aside.

Heat the peanut oil in a skillet. Add the breaded cheese to the hot oil and brown for 1 to 3 minutes on each side.

Pour the garlic sauce onto individual serving plates. Place pieces of fried cheese in the center of each pool. Sprinkle with minced parsley and serve hot.

Vella's Bear Flag

Grilling the asparagus adds an extra dimension of flavor. However, the vinaigrette is rich and substantial enough to enhance asparagus cooked in any manner.

1½ pounds medium asparagus (approximately 36 spears)
⅔ cup olive oil, plus additional oil for coating asparagus
¼ cup sherry vinegar
1¼ cups flat-leaf Italian parsley, coarsely chopped and tightly packed
½ pound Dry Jack, coarsely grated (2 cups)
Salt and pepper to taste
2 hard-boiled eggs

Snap off and discard the tough ends of the asparagus. Blanch the spears in boiling water for 1 minute, cool, and then coat with olive oil.

To prepare the vinaigrette, mix the vinegar, ⅔ cup oil, parsley, Dry Jack, salt, and pepper. Separate the whites from the yolks of the eggs and grate each separately.

Approximately 10 minutes before serving, place the asparagus spears on a hot grill. Grill for 2 or 3 minutes per side until the spears are fork-tender and lightly browned on the surface, but not burned.

Arrange on serving plates. Pour the vinaigrette over the asparagus and decorate each serving with grated egg yolk and white.

Grilled Asparagus with Dry Jack Vinaigrette

Serves 6

Vella's Bear Flag

Laura Chenel's Chèvre

❖❖❖❖❖❖❖❖❖❖❖❖

*Santa Rosa
California*

CHEESES: Various Goat
Cheeses, fresh to
aged—Crottin,
Taupinière, Tome
RETAIL SALES: Yes
TOURS: No
MAIL ORDER: Yes

Sonoma County, California, is home to nearly a hundred and fifty wineries, almost as many dairies, dozens of vegetable and fruit farms, several cheese factories, and numerous small food-processing businesses. Aside from being a food-lover's paradise, this corner of the world is blessed with an astounding diversity of terrain from redwood forests to oak-studded hills, lush valleys, and untouched ocean shores. This is the special place that we, the authors, have chosen as home.

Though I am a native of Sonoma County and have lived here most of my life, I was in my mid-twenties before I consciously chose it as my home. My city-bred parents were not particularly gifted as farmers, but they gave me a childhood in a rural setting, replete with care and feeding duties for a whole progression of animals. Nonetheless, they encouraged me to leave and educate myself so that I could teach, practice law, or join the diplomatic service. I suppose they were disconcerted when I could not bring myself to remain in any university for longer than a year at a time, was unable to focus on one specific goal, and had no idea what to make of myself. After a ten-year absence from Sonoma County, during which time I lived, studied, and worked in Europe, New York, and the San Francisco Bay Area, I returned home, still undecided about my life's direction. I was reading Adele Davis's books, eating and cooking natural foods, and eager to return to the land so that I could be self-sufficient. So I bought my first goats.

In retrospect, it was probably those goats that kept me in Sonoma County, despite my continuing wanderlust. The herd was growing, the does needed to be milked twice a day and I was becoming alarmingly attached to them. Thus, in a roundabout way, I found myself drawn to cheese making. There was all that milk and I felt responsible for it. It had to be treated with respect and be transformed into something that would pay tribute to its makers. Before long, I became aware that all my friends were goat breeders. I attended goat shows, subscribed to goat magazines, and belonged to a goat club. One could call it total immersion, I suppose. But there was no market for the milk of a small herd of goats and there was no justification for the time, money, and energy I was devoting to those charming animals.

Naturally disposed toward gardening, cooking, food preserving, and the like, I attempted to make cheese and yogurt from the abundant fresh milk. Initially, the cheese was merely an excuse to keep the goats, until I became obsessed with producing a superior cheese in quantities large enough to provide a market for the goat milk produced by all of my friends.

But my kitchen-made cheeses were not very good and the lack of information on goat-milk cheese making was discouraging. In 1979, I succumbed to a whim and traveled to France in the hope of discovering the secret of making tasty goat cheese. Quite naively (but correctly) I assumed that, once there, I would find my teachers.

Living in France was a revelation for this Sonoma County girl. During my few months there, I lived with four farmstead families in various regions and visited almost a dozen others. Each family made its own style of cheese, closely guarding the proprietary methods and nuances of technique from one another, but not from me. Every day we ate cheese with our meals. I left France with two valuable gifts: I had learned several methods of cheese making and I had gained a deep and abiding appreciation for French country life. I returned to Sonoma County determined to keep the experience alive.

Once home, I simply continued the work I had learned to love. My own cheese-making style developed, and soon I was producing and selling my first little cheeses. Not long thereafter, I took the plunge into a career of making cheese and found myself in the deep waters of renovation, transforming an old building in Santa Rosa into a state-approved plant. To ensure a milk supply, I gathered eight small-scale goat-milk producers into the fold.

Years passed. Where did they go? What happened when? It all slides together in my memory. Starting a new venture by blindly following a dream and naively believing in its successful outcome was exhilarating. That newborn business was destined to be my constant companion for years to come. I vividly remember the feeling of those days, if not the details. However, I was not, by any stretch of the imagination, a business person. Five-year plans did not enter into the picture. All I knew was that I liked making cheese. It took several years and some very tough economic lessons before I began to understand the numbers. Somehow in the process and over the years, I learned something about management—about personnel, quality control, milk supply, inventory, cash flow, equipment, and much more. My role had evolved from that of the hobbyist cheese maker to that of the manager of a small business.

Along the way, perhaps the most fortuitous and influential occurrences were all my apparently chance meetings with bright, generous, vital people, each of whom contributed something—ideas, advice, contacts, encouragement. There is a little piece of each one of these people alive right now in Laura Chenel's Chèvre.

What does the future hold? A return to the goats, for one thing. With the birth of my business, I had no choice but to give them up for a few years, and now that the business is at a more independent stage, I can direct some energy toward my new goat dairy. And I am ready for expansion into a larger, improved facility, into some exciting, very new products and into wider distribution. Of course, the business has been growing organically all along, but now its growth is conscious and directed.

There is a special pleasure in this little saga. My story, repeatedly chronicled by the media, has helped spawn an infant industry. In 1979, when I sold my first little cheeses, there were at most two others in the entire country who were also experimenting with French-style Goat Cheeses. Now there are more than fifty American farmstead or small-scale Goat Cheese companies. I believe we will witness the continued growth of this industry.

My product line started with my original fresh Goat Cheese, but for years I have also made some aged varieties, which, as the American palate has matured, have become increasingly popular. The following recipes feature two surface-ripened cheeses, Crottin and Taupinière, and one hard, aged Goat Cheese, Tome. Because they have aged, these cheeses are more complex in flavor and somewhat drier in texture than is simple, fresh Goat Cheese. A piquant, aged Goat Cheese can lend a commanding presence to a cheese course, still my favorite way to enjoy cheese. To this day, I continue to celebrate those impressionable first months in France by indulging in a selection of cheeses each evening to complete my meal.

Garlic, olive oil, fresh herbs, and Goat Cheese all abound in the South of France. Fortunately, this delightful combination is easy to prepare and enjoy in this country as well.

1 cup fruity olive oil
1 large head garlic, cloves peeled and slivered
1 large bay leaf
¼ cup fresh thyme leaves
Generous grind black pepper
5 ounces fresh Goat Cheese, thinly sliced
French bread baguette

Combine the olive oil, slivered garlic, and bay leaf in a medium sauté pan and simmer for approximately 15 minutes, but do not allow the garlic to brown. Add the thyme leaves and black pepper. Heat for 1 or 2 minutes. Arrange the cheese on a serving plate. Pour the warm garlic mixture over the cheese and serve with slices of baguette that have been warmed or toasted.

Provençal Reverie

Serves 4 to 6

Laura Chenel's Chèvre

Tomed Potatoes and Green Beans with Basil Vinaigrette

Serves 6

Chenel's Tome is a firm, dry, toothsome cheese well suited for grating. This basil dressing will enhance many salads, grilled vegetables, or meats.

1½ pounds boiling potatoes, cut into 1-inch cubes
½ pound green beans, cut into 1-inch lengths
4 ounces Tome, grated (1 cup)
15 to 20 basil leaves, minced
1 garlic clove, pressed
5 tablespoons olive oil
3 tablespoons lemon juice
Generous grind black pepper

Steam the potatoes until tender and set aside in a medium bowl.

Steam the beans until tender, plunge them into ice water to retain their color, drain, and add them to the potatoes.

In a food processor or blender, combine the Tome, basil, garlic, oil, lemon juice, and black pepper. Toss the dressing with the vegetables and serve at room temperature.

Chilly winter nights call for rich, hearty soups, robust red wine, and a blazing fireplace. This soup answers the call; each bowl sports an intensely flavored, cheese-laden topping.

    4 tablespoons butter
    4 large onions, sliced ¼-inch thick
    6 large garlic cloves, chopped
    3 cups rich chicken stock
    2 bay leaves
    1 teaspoon fresh thyme
    ½ teaspoon salt
    1 teaspoon freshly ground black pepper
    ¼ cup red wine
    2 tablespoons cognac
    4 ounces fresh Goat Cheese
    4 ounces Taupinière
    6 ½-inch-thick slices French bread, lightly toasted
    5 ounces grated Tome (1¼ cups)

In a Dutch oven melt the butter, add the onions and garlic, and sauté over medium-low heat for 30 minutes, stirring occasionally. Add the chicken stock, bay leaves, and thyme. Bring to a simmer. Mix in the wine and cognac. Add the salt and pepper. Fill individual ovenproof bowls two-thirds full with soup.

Mix together the fresh Goat Cheese and the Taupinière. Spread thickly on the toasted bread slices. Place a slice of bread on top of the soup in each bowl. Sprinkle with Tome. Place under a broiler for 1 to 2 minutes. The cheese should be lightly browned and hot, but will not appear melted. Serve immediately.

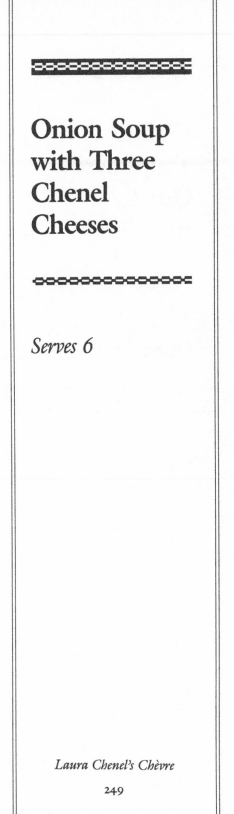

Onion Soup with Three Chenel Cheeses

Serves 6

Laura Chenel's Chèvre

Walnut and Taupinière Quick Bread

Makes 1 loaf

1 cup walnuts, chopped
2 eggs
2 tablespoons butter, melted
2 tablespoons walnut oil
1 cup buttermilk
8 ounces Taupinière (discard the rind), crumbled
2 cups all-purpose flour
½ teaspoon salt
2 teaspoons baking powder
½ teaspoon soda
1 teaspoon fresh thyme

Preheat the oven to 350°F. Toast the walnuts in the oven for 4 to 6 minutes. Cool. Leave the oven on.

Combine the eggs, butter, oil, buttermilk, and cheese. Sift together the flour, salt, baking powder, and soda. Add the thyme and the walnuts to the dry ingredients. Combine the liquid and dry ingredients, but do not overmix.

Turn into an oiled and floured bread pan. Smooth the top and decorate with 2 or 3 fresh thyme sprigs. Bake in the pre-heated oven for approximately 45 minutes. The top should be brown. Cool thoroughly before cutting.

One of our favorite combinations, asparagus, walnuts, and Goat Cheese, adds panache to pasta. Serve to six guests as a first course or to four as the main dish.

> 2 cups walnut pieces
> 1 pound dry, or 1½ pounds fresh, fettuccine
> ½ cup butter, at room temperature
> 4 garlic cloves, finely chopped
> 1 pound asparagus, trimmed, cut into 1-inch pieces, and parboiled
> 1 teaspoon salt
> Generous grind black pepper
> 2 teaspoons fresh thyme
> 4 ounces Tome, very thinly sliced
> 4 ounces Crottin, very thinly sliced

Preheat the oven to 350°F. Toast the walnuts in the oven for 4 to 6 minutes. In a large pot of boiling water cook the fettuccine al dente.

Meanwhile, melt 4 tablespoons of the butter in a medium skillet. Add the garlic and asparagus and cook for 2 minutes. Stir in the salt, pepper, and thyme. Drain the cooked pasta and toss it with the remaining 4 tablespoons butter. Toss the asparagus mixture with the pasta, cheeses, and walnuts.

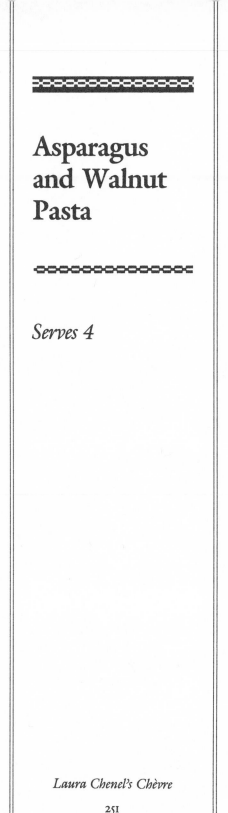

Asparagus and Walnut Pasta

Serves 4

Laura Chenel's Chèvre

Glossary of Cheese-Making Terms

▪▪▪▪▪▪▪▪▪▪▪▪▪▪▪▪▪▪▪▪▪

COAGULATION The formation of curd by the precipitation of casein, one of the proteins in milk, by acid (usually lactic acid), rennet, or microbial enzymes. Other requirements for successful coagulation and smooth gelling include correct temperature, time, and environment. Precipitation or coagulation of milk produces both a curd and the release or separation of the whey.

CULTURE (OR STARTER) A live strain of bacteria added to milk in amounts between .05 and 4.0 percent, depending upon the length of ripening time desired. As the bacteria multiply, they digest milk sugar (lactose) and produce the by-product, lactic acid, that will later, with the action of rennet, cause the formation of curd.

CURD The semi-solid product of the coagulation of milk protein.

DRAINING The process of separating the whey from the cheese curd. The speed of draining is accelerated by cutting the curd.

ENZYMES (RENNET) A protein that brings about a chemical reaction without being used up. Rennet is a proteolytic enzyme that is added to ripening milk in cheese making to form a coagulated mass. Rennets include calf rennet, an extract from the fourth stomach of a milk-fed calf, and those of microbial and vegetable origin.

MILK ACIDITY The rate of change in milk acidity is used as the primary process control in cheese making. Milk acidity is usually measured by titration and recorded as a "percentage of change in acidity" over two or more readings (over time).
    The acidity of raw milk depends on its composition (i.e., the proportions of proteins, phosphates, and salts); the acidity of milk after culture has been added is an expression of the bacterial lactic-acid production. Levels of and changes in acidity will help the cheese maker determine the quality of the milk, the speed of ripening, the addition of coagulant, and other processes.

MOLDS (FORMS) A container with holes or perforations in which the curds are placed to shape them and to allow the whey to drain off. Some cheeses are shaped by hand.

MOLD-RIPENED A mold (most commonly a *Penicillium* strain) purposely added to the milk or curd. In surface-ripened cheeses (such as Brie), the mold is allowed to grow on the surface and enzymes will penetrate to the core. In mold-injected cheeses (such as Blue), holes are punched into the cheese so that molds added to the curds can have access to oxygen and grow.

PASTEURIZATION   The process of heating milk to a high temperature and maintaining it there for an adequate amount of time to ensure that harmful and undesired bacteria are killed.

PRESSING   The process of placing soft, wet cheese curds under a slow and continuous pressure to remove the whey and minimize the loss of fat.

WHEY   An opaque, greenish-yellow fluid by-product produced in cheese manufacture. Eighty-three percent of the milk volume used ends up as whey. Because whey retains about half the nutrients of the original milk, new methods of using it are being developed. These include its use in animal feeds, carbonated beverages, and dietary foods.

For Further Information

We have merely provided a sampling of the dedicated and talented cheese makers in America today. If you are interested in knowing more about America's cheeses and cheese makers we suggest the following sources of information and include a list of the names and addresses of the cheese makers in this book.

- Local cheese shops or grocery stores, farm markets or farm organizations
- Local Chambers of Commerce and County Farm Advisors
- Restaurants that specialize in local ingredients
- Trade associations such as the Wisconsin Cheese Maker's Association and the Ohio Cheesemakers Association
- State milk and dairy food departments or Departments of Agriculture
- Barbara Lang, "A Guide to American Specialty and Farmstead Cheeses," The American Cheese Society (P.O. Box 97, Ashfield, MA 01330), 1987
- University agriculture and dairy departments

Names and Addresses of Cheese Makers

■■■■■■■■■■■■■■■■■■

F. Alleva Latticini
188 Grand Avenue
New York, New York 10013
Telephone: (212) 226-7990

Auricchio American
Route 3
Denmark, Wisconsin 54208
Telephone: (414) 863-2123

Besnier America
330 Penn Street
Belmont, Wisconsin 53510

1400 West Main Street
Turlock, California 95380
Telephone: (209) 667-4505

Bulk Farms
17487 East Lone Tree Road
Escalon, California 95320
Telephone: (209) 838-2491

Cabot Farmers' Co-op
Cabot, Vermont 05647
Telephone: (802) 563-2231

Crowley Cheese Factory
Healdville, Vermont 05758
Telephone: (802) 259-2340

Ed F. Steiner, Inc.
Baltic, Ohio 43804
Telephone: (216) 897-5505

Ferrante Cheese Company
3840 Alhambra Avenue
Martinez, California 94553
Telephone: (415) 372-9413

Goat Folks
8528 Tunison Road
Interlaken, New York 14847
Telephone: (607) 532-4343

Guilford Cheese Company
R.D. 2, Box 182
Lee Road
Guilford, Vermont 05301
Telephone: (802) 254-9182

Hawthorne Valley Farm
R.D. 2, Box 225A
Harlemville,
Ghent, New York 12075
Telephone: (518) 672-7500

Italcheese, Inc.
16919 South Broadway
Gardena, California 90248
Telephone: (213) 515-1481

Kidron Swiss Cheese Factory, Inc.
Kidron, Ohio 44636
Telephone: (216) 857-2841

Kolb-Lena Cheese Factory
3990 N. Sunnyside Road
Lena, Illinois 61048
Telephone: (815) 369-4577

Laura Chenel's Chèvre
1550 Ridley Avenue
Santa Rosa, California 95401
Telephone: (707) 575-8888

Little Rainbow Chèvre
Box 379
Rodman Road
Hillsdale, New York 12592
Telephone: (518) 325-3351

Maytag Dairy Farms
Box 806
Newton, Iowa 50208
Telephone: (800) 247-2458
in Iowa: (800) 258-2437

Mozzarella Company
2944 Elm Street
Dallas, Texas 75226
Telephone: (214) 741-4072

Mozzarella Fresca
538 Stone Road, Unit A
Benicia, California 94510
Telephone: (707) 746-6818

Mueller's Cheese House
Sugarcreek Dairy
116 Factory Street
Sugarcreek, Ohio 44681
Telephone: (216) 852-2311

Nancy's of Oregon
Springfield Creamery, Inc.
29440 Airport Road
Eugene, Oregon 97402
Telephone: (503) 689-2911

Orb Weaver Farm
Box 75
Limekiln Road
New Haven, Vermont 05472
Telephone: (802) 877-3755

Plymouth Cheese Factory
Box 1
Plymouth, Vermont 05056
Telephone: (802) 672-3650

Rawson Brook Farm
Box 345
Monterey, Massachusetts
01245
Telephone: (413) 528-2138

Rogue River Valley Creamery
311 North Front Street
Central Point, Oregon 97502
Telephone: (503) 664-2233

Shelburne Farms
Shelburne, Vermont
Telephone: (802) 985-3222

Sonoma Cheese Factory
2 Spain Street
Sonoma, California 95476
Telephone: (707) 938-5225

Tillamook County Creamery
4175 Highway 101 North
Tillamook, Oregon 97141
Telephone: (503) 842-4481

Valley View Cheese Co-op
Route 1
6519 Larson Road
South Wayne, Wisconsin
53587
Telephone: (608) 439-5569

For mail order:
Bleu Mont Dairy
10930 CTY F
Blue Mounds, Wisconsin
53517

Vella's Bear Flag
315 Second Street East
Sonoma, California 95476
Telephone: (707) 938-3232

Index

●●●●●●●●●●●●●●●●●●●●●

Cheeses appear in boldface type;
recipes, in italics.

Index

Index

Index

Index

LAURA CHENEL was born and raised in California's food- and wine-rich Sonoma County. Almost a decade ago she started her goat cheese company, Laura Chenel's Chèvre, and launched the food trend that put goat cheese on menus in most of America's fine restaurants. Named one of America's top food professionals by *Cook's Magazine* and the winner of numerous awards for her cheese, Ms. Chenel continues to produce fine cheeses in Santa Rosa, California, where she makes her home.

LINDA SIEGFRIED, a real estate broker in Sonoma County, was a talented home cook and writer and a close associate of Laura Chenel. Together they wrote *Chèvre! The Goat Cheese Cookbook* in 1983. Ms. Siegfried died in 1987, soon after the completion of the first draft of *American Country Cheese*.

EVAN JONES was born and educated in Minnesota. He has written articles for *Gourmet, Travel and Leisure,* and *The New York Times*. His books, including *American Food* and *The World of Cheese,* are considered classics. Mr. Jones resides in New York and is currently working on a biography of James Beard.

0398